Sakuma Shozan

佐久間象山

Record of Conscience

省諐録

By Daisuke Konno

紺野大介

佐久間象山（1811〜1864）
Sakuma Shozan

目次
Contents

1. まえがき 4
   (Introduction)

2. 序章：佐久間象山の概要 26
   (Overview of Sakuma Shozan)

3. 省諐録：原文 88
   (Original text by Chinese classical literature)

4. 本章：『省諐録』逐語訳：英訳 131
   (Main course："Record of Conscience")

5. 跋文（国際日本文化研究センター名誉教授・笠谷和比古博士）... 192
   (Contribution by Dr. Kazuhiko Kasaya)

6. 引用および参考文献 200
   (Bibliography and References)

まえがき

　佐久間象山著作の『省警録』(Record of Conscience)は、筆者にとり第一作目の橋本左内著作『啓発録』英訳書（Treatise on Enlightenment）及び第二作目の吉田松陰著作『留魂録』英訳書（Soulful Minute）に続く、第三作目の英訳書である。

　『啓発録』は、橋本左内（1834～1859）が15歳（満14歳）の時に、偉人英傑の伝記を読み、古人の言行・節義を学んで深く感奮興起し、自己の規範として、自らを鞭撻するために著したものであり、左内の一生は本書を出発点として展開されたものといって過言でないであろう。このような書物が古来、15歳の少年をして草された類例は、筆者の知る限り古今東西なく、門弟の溝口辰五郎（後の加藤斌{ナカバ}）、実弟の橋本綱常、越前藩儒の矢島立軒を経由、土佐藩士で後に宮内大臣となった田中光顕伯爵の手にわたり、同氏より宮内省に献納され、現在は皇室の所蔵品である「御物」として今日に至っている。

　『留魂録』は、吉田松陰（1830～1859）が安政の大獄で処刑される前日のほぼ丸一日の24時間、獄中で書き上げた遺書である。薄葉半紙を四つ折りにした縦12cm、横17cm、19面を細書きにした約5000字は、不自由な獄舎のものとはいえ、死を目前にした人間とは思えないほどの冷静さで決別の辞が述べられており、門人への激励や周囲への細心の配慮がなされている。
『留魂録』は、松陰を師と仰ぐ幕末の志士達に{聖書}として作用し、"明治維新"という自分たちの手で勝ち取った新時代を構築し、新しい日本を主導した礎の一つとなった。

　橋本左内は満25歳、吉田松陰は満29歳で、井伊直弼による「安政の大獄」で処刑された。

Introduction

Seikenroku ("Record of Conscience") by Sakuma Shozan is the third work I have translated into English, after the first, *Keihatsuroku* ("Treatise on Enlightenment") by Hashimoto Sanai, and the second, *Ryūkonroku* ("Soulful Minute") by Yoshida Shoin.

Hashimoto Sanai (1834-1859) wrote "Treatise on Enlightenment" when he was fourteen years old. He had read the biographies of great men, studied the words, deeds and morality of the ancients, and was deeply inspired by them. He then wrote "Treatise on Enlightenment" as his own moral code for self-encouragement. In fact, it would be no exaggeration to say that Sanai's whole life development started from this book. To my knowledge, there is no other example in any time or place of such a work being written by a youth of only fourteen. The work passed into the hands of his follower Mizoguchi Tatsugoro (later Kato Nakaba), who gave it to Sanai's brother Hashimoto Tsunatsune, and he in turn to the Echizen Confucian scholar Yajima Ryuken. Finally, it came into the possession of Count Mitsuaki Tanaka, a samurai from the Tosa Domain who was to become Minister of the Imperial Household. Tanaka donated it to the Imperial Household Ministry, where it survives to this day as an "Imperial Treasure".

"Soulful Minute" is a testament written over the course of one whole day by Yoshida Shoin (1830-1859). He wrote it in prison before his execution the following day as part of the Ansei Purge. "Soulful Minute" consists of around 5,000 characters written finely on 19 pages of thin *hanshi* paper folded in four, measuring 12cm long by 17cm wide. In it, Yoshida sets down his final words with a composure belying the fact that he was awaiting death, and in spite of the constraints placed on his freedom in prison. He expresses words of encouragement to his followers and shows caring consideration to those around him.

"Soulful Minute" had the effect of a "bible" on the late-Edo patriots who looked up to Shoin as a mentor. They used it as a foundation stone for their leadership of the new Japan and for building the new era now known as the "Meiji Restoration", which they had won through their own deeds.

Hashimoto Sanai was executed at the age of 25, and Yoshida Shoin at 29, as part of the Ansei Purge orchestrated by Ii Naosuke.

By contrast to both of these, "Record of Conscience" by Sakuma Shozan (1811-1864) was set down over a period of nine years while he was under house arrest in Matsushiro. Unlike Hashimoto's "Treatise on

さて佐久間象山（1811～1864）の『省響録』は松代に蟄居中の９年間で記録したもので、橋本左内『啓発録』、吉田松陰『留魂録』の著作と異なり、所謂、壮年期のものである。すなわち『省響録』は、象山が弟子の吉田松陰の密航渡海事件に連座して投獄された際、獄中で腹案を練った感想録の色彩が強い。

　しかし『省響録』は単なる獄中の所感録ではなく、ペリー来航を中心とした政治体制の危機と国体の在り方に関する既往の回顧があり、修養論あり、学問観あり、経世論あり、海防論等々57ヶ条に及んでおり、象山の学問・思想の集大成と見ることができる。また当時の国防を知る上で歴史的に貴重な作品である。

　『省響録』は、元来は過ちを省りみるの記、との意味である。しかし象山は、過ちを省みるどころか、強い自負の念と使命感に基づき、自分の目で見た体験、見たものの本質、その時の時勢についての思想や先見性について率直に述べており、自己の思念や考え方の正当性を強調し、その思想を述べた論説集となっているといえよう。そして出獄後メモとして残しておいたものを基に、安政年代の蟄居中に纏めたのである。『省響録』は前言に記されている通りであるとすれば、子孫にその生き様を示す為であり、出版して広く世間に示すためではない、とある。事実、これが出版されたのは象山が京都で暗殺された元治元年（1864年）以降の、明治５年（1872年）になってからであり、象山の正妻・お順の兄であった勝海舟（1823～1899）が百二十両（現在の600万円相当）の費用を負担して出版されたものである。

　佐久間象山｛通称、幼名；啓之助、元服後：修理（しゅり）、実名である諱（いみな）は国忠（くにただ）、その後、啓（ひらき），字（あざな）は子迪（してき）その後、子明（しめい）を用いた｝の世界観は、いわば朱子学へ一途に突き進み、その傾倒振りなどからも思想的には極めて保守的であったと言えよう。少し乱暴な言い方が許されるとしたら、幕末期にあって例えば、橋本左内が十代半ばにも拘らず、若さを超越した炯眼で、当時の崩れゆく政治体制における大人の世界の不条理を洞察し冷静に見通していたのに対し、朱子学にのめり込んでいった象山は三十代に入ってから世の中、何処か変である、と分かった人物でもある。

Enlightenment" and Yoshida's "Soulful Minute", moreover, "Record of Conscience" was written when its author was in late middle age. "Record of Conscience" has a strong flavour of a collection of thoughts planned in prison, after Shozan had been incarcerated for complicity in a stowaway incident involving his follower Yoshida Shoin. But "Record of Conscience" is not merely a record of thoughts written in prison, for it contains 57 sections on a variety of subjects including historical retrospection on the crisis facing Japan's political system and the state of the national polity (with particular reference to the Perry Expedition), doctrine on human cultivation, scholarship, a treatise on state affairs, and a theory of naval defence. It is a veritable compendium of Shozan's learning and thought. It is also a work of great historical value as an aid to understanding the state of Japan's national defence at that time.

In itself, the title 省譽録 (*Seikenroku*) means a written reflection on errors committed. But far from reflecting on errors, Shozan candidly states thoughts and predictions regarding things he has personally experienced, the true essence of things he has seen, and the circumstances of the times, based on a strong sense of pride and mission. Indeed, "Record of Conscience" could be described as a collection of essays in which Shozan asserts the validity of his own thoughts and ideas and expresses his doctrine. He summarized these thoughts and ideas while in confinement during the Ansei era, based on notes jotted down after his release from prison. If "Record of Conscience" were as described in its introduction, its purpose would have been to show his descendants how they should live their lives, rather than being published and widely disclosed to society at large. In fact, it was not published until 1872, after Shozan's assassination in Kyoto in 1864. It was Katsu Kaishu (1823-1899), elder brother of Shozan's wife O-Jun, who paid the fee of 120 *ryō* to have it published.

Though commonly known as Sakuma Shozan, "Shozan" was in fact a pseudonym. His childhood name was Keinosuke. On reaching adulthood, he was also called Shuri, but his real name was Kunitada, later changing to Hiraki. His courtesy name was initially Shiteki, but this again later changed to Shimei.

In terms of his world view, Sakuma Shozan was single-mindedly devoted to Neo-Confucianism. And from the nature of his commitment to this philosophy, we could say that he was ideologically very conservative. If a somewhat crude comparison might be permitted, near the end of the Edo period, Hashimoto Sanai saw through the absurdity of the adult world in the crumbling political system of the day, and calmly made prognostications with a sharp insight that belied his youth.

他方で、象山の「東洋の道徳、西洋の芸術（＝技術）」の名言で推察できるように、西洋の科学技術そのものに頗る強い関心を示した。象山は、数量化するセンスが高く、左脳というか、理系脳が他の幕末期の志士達に比し頗る豊かであった。この何でも数量化する、という考え方や振る舞い、行動は、科学技術のための基本姿勢である。この視座からも象山は幕末維新期で特筆すべき最右翼の人物であったと言えよう。

　周知の通り、近代日本の歴史の沸騰点といわれる幕末維新期には、生活の価値観が一変した。黒船来航に代表されるように、鎖国から開国にむけて門閥政治と幕藩体制下の混乱に基づく国家的危機に際し、誰がどう振舞ったか？これを知るため先ず藤田東湖、渡辺崋山、佐久間象山、横井小楠、大塩平八郎、高野長英、吉田松陰、橋本左内、西郷隆盛、高杉晋作、桂小五郎、河井継之助、小林虎三郎、坂本龍馬、江藤新平らの事績をよく調査する。その上で史実に基づいた検討や考察を加えると、現在の一般社会において、小説（Fiction）やTVドラマ等の行き過ぎた脚色のため、実物以上に過大評価されている人物と、過小評価されている人物が見えてくる。管見にすぎないが、後者の過小評価されている筆頭が佐久間象山である＿＿＿と愚考している。

　本書『省響録』英訳に際し、過去の象山評価の幾つかの証左を示した。贅言を費やすまでもなく、佐久間象山に関する著書や『省録響』逐語訳、意訳書などの解説者の見解はそれぞれ興味深く、その意味するところは深長で大きい。

　個人的には特に巻末に示した文献2.に見える飯島忠夫、文献4.に見える宮本仲、文献9.に見る植手通有、文献12.に示した松浦玲の象山考察は省察的内容で感慨深い。これらは各文献を読んで戴く他はなく、象山に関する多大な見解と考察が述べられている。それでも尚というべきか、それだからこそというべきか、本書の「前書き」としては、それ以外の過去・現在の碩学、泰斗が俯瞰的に、あるいは概括的に象山の事績を様々な角度から言及しているので少し触れてみる。

This was despite the fact that he was only in his mid-teens. By contrast, Shozan, immersed in Neo-Confucianism, only saw that something was wrong with the world when he was in his thirties. On the other hand, as can be gleaned from Shozan's famous phrase "Eastern ethics, Western technical learning", he had a very strong interest in western science and technology. He seems to have had a strong affinity for quantification; his science brain, or perhaps his left brain, was extremely rich compared to other patriots near the end of the Edo period. This rationale, behaviour or guiding principle of quantifying everything is the basic attitude required of science and technology. From this perspective, too, Shozan could be described as a most noteworthy figure in the "Bakumatsu" or final Edo period.

As is well known, Japanese lifestyle values were utterly transformed in that period of transition from the final days of the Tokugawa shogunate to the Meiji Restoration – a period regarded as the boiling point of modern Japanese history. But who did what in those days of national crisis, based on confusion under pedigree politics and the shogunate system as Japan emerged from national seclusion, illustrated by the arrival of Commodore Perry and his "Black Ships"? To answer that question, the exploits of Fujita Toko, Watanabe Kazan, Sakuma Shozan, Yokoi Shonan, Oshio Heihachiro, Takano Choei, Yoshida Shoin, Hashimoto Sanai, Saigo Takamori, Takasugi Shinsaku, Katsura Kogoro, Kawai Tsuginosuke, Kobayashi Torasaburo, Sakamoto Ryoma, Eto Shinpei and others are often researched. If we go on to investigate these figures based on their historical reality, we find that some historical personalities have been overvalued compared to their reality while others have been undervalued, owing to excessive dramatization in novels (fiction), TV dramas and others in society at large today. My personal view is that Sakuma Shozan tops the list of the undervalued.

In producing this English translation of *Seikenroku*, I have uncovered several examples showing how Shozan has been evaluated in the past. Of course, the opinions of commentators in books about Sakuma Shozan, as well as literal and liberal translations of *Seikenroku*, are all deeply interesting and highly significant in their own right. Personally, I find the investigation of Shozan by Tadao Iijima in Bibliography Reference 2, Chu Miyamoto in Reference 4, Michiari Uete in Reference 9 and Rei Matsuura in Reference 12 particularly evocative with their keenly inquiring content. I would invite the reader to take a look at these works, as they include a great volume of opinion and analysis concerning Shozan. But in spite of these, or perhaps because of them, I will also touch on other scholars and authorities past

古くは徳富蘇峰(1863-1954)がその著作『吉田松陰』(文献 46.)において、佐久間象山と横井小楠を比較している。小楠が実学を詠い直観的な活眼活学に基づく「経世論的実学思想」の師であったのに対し、象山は易理に通じ、聖学を講明し、心に大道を知る、解剖学的、大建築師的な「海防論的実学思想」の師であったとしている。小楠が『国是七条』で天理人情の大妙理を看取し開国論を唱えたのに対し、象山は『海防八策』において、国防軍備の大経綸により無謀攘夷の非を論じ、主として論理と分析から科学技術の知見を最大限に広めようとした、としている。

　東洋史研究を基盤として近代歴史学を主導した宮崎市定(1901-1995)は、「幕末の攘夷論と開国論」(文献 54.)の中で佐久間象山について次のように言及している。
「日本の幕末維新史は、長い間いわゆる明治の元勲たちの圧迫を受けて、非常に歪んだ形で述べられてきた。戦後になっても一度ゆがんだ形は、なかなか真の姿が取り戻せない。いわゆる攘夷運動というものの実態も、意外に真相が知られていないのではあるまいか。そしてこれが分かっていない限り、せっかく一死を賭して開国論を唱えた佐久間象山の歴史上の位置付けも十分に満たされない恐れがある」として佐久間象山暗殺の背景を深く考察している。
「中でも薩長のような、運営資金としての金ヅルを持たない山国・信州から出た象山のような政客は、哀れなものであった。あくまで真っ正直な開国論で、いわば汚い攘夷論に立ち向かう。それは殆ど単身素手で、組織ある暴力団の真ん中へ飛び込むようなものであった。その立場は勢い既成に従って、世界の変化に追いつこうとする公武合体の開国論を唱えるより他策が無かったのである」＿＿として象山擁護を響かせながら、その立ち位置を明確にしている。

　また横井小楠研究者として知られる近世日本思想史家・東北大学名誉教授・源了圓(1920-)は、「佐久間象山・幕末の群像第8巻」(文献 57.)等において、

and present in my "Introduction" to this publication. This is because they mention Shozan's achievements from a variety of angles, whether in detail or more generally.

For example, Soho Tokutomi (1863-1954) compared Sakuma Shozan with Yokoi Shonan in his book *Yoshida Shōin* (see Ref. 46). In it, he asserts that, while Shonan espoused practical science and was a master of "the doctrine of practical science led by opinion" based on intuitive insight and active knowledge, Shozan was well-versed in divination, expounded the truths of Confucianism, and knew the essence of virtue; he was a master of the anatomical, grand-architect style "doctrine of practical science led by naval defence policy". And while Shonan perceived the true righteousness of the laws of nature and humanity and advocated an end to Japan's isolation in his *Kokuze Shichijō* ("Seven Articles of State Policy"), Shozan, in *Kaibō Hassaku* ("Eight Measures for Naval Defence"), argued against the reckless expulsion of foreigners based on the major tenet of arming for national defence. Instead, he tried to spread knowledge on science and technology to the maximum extent possible, mainly by using logic and analysis.

Ichisada Miyazaki (1901-1995), who led the study of modern history founded on oriental history research, writes the following about Sakuma Shozan in his "*Bakumatsu no Jōiron to Kaikokuron*" (Bakumatsu Theories of Expelling Foreigners and Westernization; see Ref. 54).

"For a long time, Japan's history from the end of the Edo period to the Meiji Restoration has been described in a very distorted form, influenced by pressure from the so-called elder statesmen of the Meiji period. And once distorted, this form has not been easy to correct, even since the war.

For example, surprisingly little is known of the truth behind the so-called *jōi* or "expel foreigners" movement. And without that truth being known, Sakuma Shozan, a man who risked his life to advocate the end of Japan's isolation, might be deprived of his rightful place in history. For that reason, I will closely examine the background to Sakuma Shozan's assassination.

Shozan hailed from the mountainous province of Shinshu, which (unlike Satsuma and Choshu) lacked the financial means required to fund its activities. This placed Shozan in a pitiful position as a political activist. He opposed the "dirty" Jōi movement with his honest insistence on ending national isolation. It was like jumping into the midst of a criminal gang, alone and unarmed. In his position, the only path

人物としての横井小楠と佐久間象山を、その思想・理念、生き様などを比較している。その中で小楠に比し、象山の気風や性格に対し幾分批判的ながらも、同時代、同世代、指導者としてほぼ同格の立場で、江戸周辺の同場所で生きたにもかかわらず一度も相対す機会がなかった模様の二人の巨人に対し以下のように述べている。象山の著作の中で、特に藩士や子弟に朱子学を学ばせ、同時に蘭学・砲術なども取り入れた「学政意見書並びに藩老に呈する附書」を上書した内容について、「象山の上書の第一号が、教育に関するものであったこと、このことは象山が、幕末に必要な諸処の改革において、教育改革こそが根本課題である、と考えていたことを物語るといえよう」＿＿と国体の要諦について付言している。

　また政治学者・哲学者である丸山眞男(1914-1996)は、1965年5月号の『展望』第77号、"幕末における視座の変革"(文献83.)において以下のように述べている。「象山は幕末の危機的状況の中で、世界の新しい認識の必要、旧来の世界像を変えていく必要を説いたとし、世界を知るには我々自身の既成の眼鏡、伝統的な概念装置を吟味しなければ本当の問題が何処にあるかは分からない」と論説。象山が獲得した「知識の質」を言及した。正統派朱子学者であった象山が、西洋の科学技術の重要性に気づき、それを少しづつ受容していく過程は、我国の人々が「近代」というものをどのように把握したかを示す最も典型的な例と指摘した。そして象山がヨーロッパの科学的方法を何処まで理解していたかということよりも、考え方の進んで行く方向が、何処に向いていたかという点が極めて大事なのである。すなわち象山は何処までも朱子学の精神に従い、それを媒介としてヨーロッパの自然科学を勉強して行く＿＿。まさにその過程が、朱子学を含めた漢学の枠を突き破っていく過程であった。そして科学技術の把握の様子について、ヨーロッパの自然科学の基礎には、「万学の基本としての詳証術(=数学)があることを予感していた」として高い評価を与えた。

available was to abide by existing convention and advocate a policy of ending isolation through a union of civil and military government, in order to keep pace with changes in the world." In this way, Miyazaki makes Shozan's position clear while spelling out the case for his defence.

Minamoto Ryoen (1920-), Emeritus Professor of Tohoku University and a commentator on the history of modern Japanese thought, is known for his research on Yokoi Shonan. In works such as *Sakuma Shōzan: Bakumatsu Ishin no Gunzō Dai Hachi Kan* (Sakuma Shozan: Group Portrait from the Bakumatsu and Meiji Restoration Vol. 8; see Ref. 57), he compares the ideas, philosophies, lifestyles and other personal aspects of Yokoi Shonan with those of Sakuma Shozan. Though somewhat critical of Shozan's ethos and character in comparison to Shonan, he makes various statements about these two contemporary giants who, despite living in the same era, being of the same generation, enjoying a very similar status as leaders and living in the same location near Edo, never had the opportunity to meet. Of Shozan's works, he particularly focuses on his teaching of Neo-Confucianism to clansmen and youngsters and his submission of an "Opinion on Educational Policy and Memorandum Presented to the Clan Elders" incorporating both Dutch studies and gunnery. On the essence of the national polity, he remarks that "Shozan's first submission was related to education. This would seem to show that Shozan, in the various reforms that were needed in the Bakumatsu period, saw reform of education in itself as the fundamental issue."

Meanwhile, the political scientist and philosopher Masao Maruyama (1914-1996) discussed Sakuma Shozan in his essay *Bakumatsu ni Okeru Shiza no Henkaku* ("Changing Perspectives in the Bakumatsu Period"; see Ref. 83) in Issue 77 of *Tenbō* (May 1965). Amid the state of crisis as the Tokugawa shogunate drew to an end, Shozan advocated the need for a new perception of the world and the need to change the traditional world view; he explained that, in order to know the world, the true location of the problem would only be discovered by examining one's own existing glasses and traditional conceptual devices. Maruyama also mentions the "quality of knowledge" acquired by Shozan. He points out that the process whereby Shozan, as an orthodox Neo-Confucianist, recognized the importance of western science and technology and gradually accepted it is the most typical example of how people in Japan grasped "modernity". A very important point here is the direction in which Shozan's thoughts were progressing, rather than how far he understood European scientific methods. That is, "Shozan

また近代日本精神史の思想家・松本健一(1946-)は、その著『評伝 佐久間象山』(文献 11.)において、象山の人間性を深く分厚く、弾力性を持って考察し以下のように述べている。象山の本質は革命家ではなく思想家、であること、政治家では無論なく、幕末の開国思想それ自体のラディカル(急進的)さによって、革命思想家という時代的役割を担わされたと考察しており、その証左として『省䙅録』の要諦を詳しく分析している。また誤解、正解を含めて人口に膾炙している象山の自信過剰、傲岸不遜あるいは勝海舟の言う「法螺吹き論」との関係においても、その内容に触れている。象山のホラは、彼の思想の先駆性や歴史的 perspective（物事を見通す釣合の取れた見方）の確かさを、当時は誰も理解できなかったことから、ホラではないかと思われていた節がある、としている。すなわち彼が『省䙅録』で清国の魏源を批判したことや、下田開港論を唱えた江川太郎左衛門（坦庵）を批判して、横浜開港論を述べたこと、日本で洋式大砲を作れるのは自分一人だといったことなどは、いずれも歴史によってその正しさが証明されるのである、と述べており、勝海舟の自信の強さも時に辟易させられるとして象山を擁護している。いずれにせよ象山の『省䙅録』は、西洋文明を、"全て自ら経験し、作っていく"ことで西洋に対抗せんとする、近代日本の基本戦略を形作っていったのである、と結言している。

　また自然科学の視点から幕末期の科学技術面を研究した弘前大学教授の東徹(1953-)は、事実上の学位論文ともいうべき「佐久間象山と科学技術」(文献 16.)の中で以下のように述べている。佐久間象山が「およそ事は自から之を為さずして、能く其の要領を得る者は之なし」と強調し、実際に様々な「モノ」を作ろうとした。
この意味で象山は幕末のこの時代に科学者(Scientist)と技術者(Engineer)の視座を有していた。象山の発言には、「知識」と「実践」に係わる内容が重要なキーワードであり、当時の我が国の人々が、西洋の技術を本気で移植しようとした時の分析対象として、佐久間象山は落とすことができない存在といえる、と述べている。すなわち「東洋の道徳、西洋の技術」の中の、知識と技術の実践を日

remained faithful to the spirit of Neo-Confucianism and studied European natural sciences through this as a medium. This was truly a process of breaking through the framework of Chinese learning, including Neo-Confucianism." And Maruyama gives high praise to Shozan's grasp of science and technology, writing "He felt intuitively that what he called "probative science (= mathematics) as the basis of all science" lay at the foundation of European natural sciences.

Another commentator is Kenichi Matsumoto (1946–), a thinker of modern Japanese intellectual history. In his book *Hyōden Sakuma Shōzan* (see Ref. 11), he examines Shozan's humanity with depth, breadth and flexibility. He discusses how Shozan's true nature was as a thinker, not a revolutionary, and of course not as a politician; and how, due to the radical nature of the Bakumatsu policy to end Japan's isolation, he was made to shoulder the contemporary role of a revolutionary thinker. As proof of that, Matsumoto analyzes the essence of "Record of Conscience" in detail. He also touches on its content in relation to Shozan's presumptuousness and haughty irreverence, or what Katsu Kaishu calls his "trumpet-blowing doctrine" – characteristics that are universally praised in common parlance, whether correctly or mistakenly understood. He says there is a theory that Shozan's "trumpet" was only seen as such because nobody at the time could understand the pioneering nature of his thought or the certainty of his historical perspective (i.e. his balanced insight into the reality of things). Specifically, Matsumoto asserts that Shozan's criticism of Qing China's Wei Yuan in "Record of Conscience", his criticism of Egawa Tarozaemon (or Tannan, who advocated opening Shimoda Port) and support for the policy of opening Yokohama Port, and his claim to be the only person in Japan who could manufacture western-style cannon have all been proved correct by history. He defends Shozan, and is sometimes annoyed by the strength of Katsu Kaishu's confidence. In any case, he concludes that Shozan's "Record of Conscience" helped shape modern Japan's basic strategy of trying to compete with the west by "experiencing and reproducing Western civilization by ourselves".

Toru Azuma, a professor at Hirosaki University, has researched science and technology in the Bakumatsu period from the viewpoint of natural sciences. He states the following in *Sakuma Shozan to Kagaku Gijutsu* ("Sakuma Shozan, Science and Technology"; see Ref. 16), which could be described as his graduation thesis. He asserts that Sakuma Shozan actually tried to make various "objects" by himself, because "the

本へ導入しなければならないと感じ、例えば機械工学の基礎である「力学」という学問に言及した。「コロンビュスが究理の力を以って新世界を見出し、コペルニキュスが地動の説を発明し、ネウトンが重力引力の実理を究知し、三大発明以来万般の学術皆其れ根底を得、虚誕の筋なくしばし皆著実に相成り」というように、象山の視界も科学の領域まで拡大したことは確実である。一方、視界が拡大することと、そこで一定の理解を得ることとは別問題とし、その状況の調査、また地球科学的な事項を主内容とするソンメル(J.G.Sommer)の著した究理書などを取り上げ、象山の「知識」の内容、蘭書を基にした電気治療機の製作という「実践」した分析と検討を試みている。こうした考究のもと、象山を理解するには、象山の世界観が自然科学的には革新的でありながら政治的に非常に保守的であること、真理の体系の中で朱子学と格物究理に突き進んで行ったこと、即ち、本来相容れないものを、半ば強引に橋をかけようとした象山の、何処がブレていたかを分かってあげる必要がある、としている。

　筆者は昔、「木曽路はすべて山の中にある」という序章ではじまる文豪・島崎藤村の名著『夜明け前』を学生時代に読んだことがある。若い学生にとり序章がかなり冗長に感じ、決してなじみやすくなかった。
　周知のとおり、本書は木曽路の山中にありながら幕末維新期の時代の動きを追跡する、藤村の父親である「青山半蔵」の生涯を描いたファミリーヒストリーである。国学に心傾ける青山半蔵が、黒船来襲で政治運動への参加を願う心と、本陣・問屋・庄屋を兼ねる旧家の仕事に挟まれながら、歴史は半蔵の目前で刻々と移り変わっていく。藤村が父を題材に幕末・明治維新に生きた一人の人間のモデルを描きながら自己を凝視した畢生の大作。官軍と旧幕府軍の激しい戦い、官軍の勝利、江戸から東京へと名称変更など、ありとあらゆるものが新しく作り変えられていく中で、結局、明治新政府は半蔵の夢みていたものでなかった。維新後も生活の基点、人々の暮らしの視点でみると幕末期と一体何が変わったか夢破れていく物語・作品であり、政治体制の変革と庶民生活の乖離を深く印象付けたものである。

essential nature of objects cannot easily be understood unless we make them ourselves".

In this sense, Shozan adopted the viewpoint of a scientist and an engineer in this Bakumatsu period. In remarks by Shozan, Azuma finds important keywords in his discussion of "knowledge" and "practice", and suggests that Shozan is indispensable as a subject for analysis at a time when the Japanese seriously wanted to transplant Western technology. That is to say, in his "Eastern ethics, Western technical learning", Shozan felt that knowledge and technical practice should be introduced into Japan; for example, he mentioned the academic discipline of "dynamics", the basis of mechanical engineering. As Shozan himself wrote, "Columbus discovered the New World by using the power of scientific inquiry, Copernicus devised the theory of planetary motion, and Newton elucidated the principle of gravity. Since these three discoveries were made, they have become the foundation of all science, so that we can now explain all phenomena without recourse to nonsense". This makes it plain that Shozan's viewpoint extended to the realm of science. On the other hand, Azuma points to investigative works by J.G.Sommer, which suggest that expanding one's viewpoint is not necessarily the same as reaching an understanding. Instead, these works mainly concern research on that situation and matters related to earth sciences. In this light, Azuma attempts to analyze and study the content of Shozan's "knowledge" and his "practice" in making an electric therapy machine based on western studies. Based on this kind of elaboration, he says that in order to understand Shozan, we should appreciate that his world view was politically very conservative, despite his innovative attitude to natural sciences. We should also understand the uncertainty faced by Shozan, who thrust himself into both Neo-Confucianism and investigative inquiry in a truth-based system, and almost forcibly tried to build a bridge between these two inherently incompatible pursuits.

Long ago, as a student, I read the famous work *Yoakemae* ("Before the Dawn") by the renowned writer Toson Shimazaki. The Preface to this work opens with the phrase *Kisoji wa subete yama no naka de aru* ("The entire Kisoji is in the mountains"). For a young student, the Preface seemed quite tedious, and it was not at all easy to feel at home with the book.

As is well known, *Yoakemae* is a family history depicting the life of Toson's father, "Aoyama Hanzo". Set in the mountains of Kisoji, it traces movements in the days between the end of the Tokugawa shogunate and the Meiji Restoration. Aoyama Hanzo is absorbed in his study of Japanese classics, but with the arrival of Perry's "black ships", he is

一方、『省響録』本文中では、個人的には吉田松陰の密航渡海事件に連座し罪を得た時の想いを述べた個所など最も感慨が深い。即ち、「吾この境を履まざれば、この省覚なし。一跌を経なければ一知を長ずとは、果たして虚語にあらず」（意訳すれば、自分は今回の体験をして初めて今日のような悟りに達した。人間、一度つまずけば、一つの知を得るとは、本当のことである）。この文章は「響を省みる、と言いながらも、自分は為すべきことを為すべきときに為した。従って何時死んでもよく、評価は後世の公論が必ず支持してくれるだろう」——と強調し、現代の人々の様々な場面への教訓とさせている。以上こうした感慨を含め、『啓発録』や『留魂録』英完訳を踏まえつつ全体を俯瞰すると、象山という一人の思想家が赤裸々に記録した『省響録』の歴史的価値は小さくなく、日本人のエートスの長短を理解する上で、現代にも大きな示唆を与えているといえよう。

　さて過去の日本語の『省響録』紹介や解説は、巻末文献に示したように、信濃教育会編集の象山全集第一巻の『省響録』（昭和9年7月発行）、宮本仲著『佐久間象山』（岩波版）{象山社}の附録『省響録』（昭和7年2月発行）、佐久間象山著・飯島忠夫訳注『省響録』（岩波文庫版 昭和44年4月発行）、日本思想体系55『渡辺崋山　高野長英　佐久間象山　横井小楠　橋本左内』（岩波書店）（昭和46年6月発刊）の中の『省響録』（植手通有校注）、倉田信久著『詳解　省慾録』（平成元年8月発行）、松浦玲責任編集『佐久間象山・横井小楠』（中央公論社）の中の『省響録』（昭和59年6月発行）など、現在まで多大な貢献やご尽力があった。

　これ等に対し、橋本左内著『啓発録』、吉田松陰著『留魂録』同様、先ず象山の『省響録』原文をよく読み語義を確かめ訓読した。その後、逐語訳することになるわけであるが既に多くの逐語訳が存在する。従って現在となっては、逐語訳も各々細かな差異が認められるものの大同小異であり、本書では原文を巻末の文献の1．信濃教育会編を導入・転記させて戴いた。また逐語訳は文献9．の日本思想大系55を引用させて戴き、英語圏の読者、日本の一般読者の利便性を

caught between a desire to join a political movement and his work in the family business, which combines an inn for government officials with a wholesale store and the village headman's office. In the process, history changes moment by moment before Hanzo's eyes. This is an epic life story full of self-examination, using Toson's father as model to portray life during the change from the Edo period to the Meiji Restoration. Fierce fighting between imperial forces and the old shogunate army results in victory for the former, after which the name of the capital is changed from Edo to Tokyo and all manner of things are replaced with the new. But after all, the new Meiji government was not what Hanzo had dreamt of. This is a story of broken dreams, asking what had actually changed after the Restoration compared to the Edo period, in terms of the basics of living and people's daily lives. In the process, it gives a deep impression of the detachment between changes in political systems and ordinary people's lives.

"Record of Conscience", on the other hand, evokes a strong sense of deep emotion, especially in the passage where Shozan recalls his feelings on being punished for complicity in the Yoshida Shoin stowaway incident (Section 7). For he writes, "I reached my current mental attitude for the first time after my experience in jail. It is true that we learn from our mistakes." To paraphrase this and other passages, Shozan declares that "Though I speak of looking back on errors, I did what I had to do when I had to do it. Therefore, I am ready to die at any time, and public opinion in future generations will surely support me." So saying, he wants to turn his experience into a lesson to be learnt by his contemporaries in various situations. Seen in its entirety, including this kind of deep emotion, and in comparison to "Treatise on Enlightenment" and "Soulful Minute", "Record of Conscience" is of no small historical value, in that it is a frank record set down by Shozan as a thinker of his day. Indeed, it could also be said to provide valuable suggestions for the present day, in understanding the background to the Japanese ethos.

Great contributions and efforts have already been made in Japanese-language publications and commentaries on *Seikenroku*, as listed in the bibliography at the end of this book. These include *Seikenroku* in Vol. 1 of the "Complete Works of Shozan" edited by the Shinano Kyoiku Kai (published in July 1934), *Seikenroku* in the Appendix to *Sakuma Shōzan* (Iwanami edition, Shozansha) by Chu Miyamoto (February 1932), *Seikenroku* by Sakuma Shozan, translated with notes by Tadao Iijima (Iwanami Bunko, April 1969), *Seikenroku* (annotated by Michiari Uete) in *Watanabe Kazan, Takano Chōei, Sakuma Shōzan, Yokoi Shōnan, Hashimoto Sanai*, Nihon Shisō Taikei

図ったつもりでいる。また意訳については既に多く解説付きで上梓されている。本書では原文、逐語訳、英訳を併記して読者の参考に供するよう努めた。この場をお借りし先人のご努力に心からの敬意を表したい。

尚、「佐久間象山 雅号呼称の決め手」（文献78.）と題した信州大学教養学部紀要に基づき、特に断らない場合「ぞうざん:Zouzan」ではなく「しょうざん:Shozan」で統一した。また佐久間象山を知らない主として英語圏を中心とした諸外国の方々に関心を持って戴くために、佐久間象山に関連した書簡、書状、自筆文稿、意見書、書画、絵巻、秘図なども比較的多く取り上げ、視覚に訴えるよう努めた。これらの出典は巻末ほか随所に明記したつもりでいる。また各頁に逐一出典掲載を省略しているが、主として真田宝物館・象山記念館の『佐久間象山の世界』、『佐久間象山と象山神社』、『松代藩と黒船来航』、『真田家の科学技術』を底本として使用させていただいており、ここに深い感謝の意を表します。

『省諐録』の英完訳は筆者の調査する限り、未だ発表されていない。情報検索で調べた範囲では、1957年に米国 Columbia 大学において、Charles Terry が「Sakuma Shozan and His Seikenroku」というタイトルで修士論文を発表している。この抄訳が Sources of Japanese Tradition (Columbia University Press 2005, P.633〜638) に認められるが、象山の思想の紹介に『省諐録』が部分的材料として使われており、完訳になっているわけではない。このことをドイツのハイデルベルグ大学・元日本研究所長の Wolfgang Schamoni 名誉教授・文学博士からご教示戴き、参考になりました。お礼申し上げます。

55 (Iwanami Shoten, June 1971), *Shōkai Seikenroku* ("Record of Conscience: A Detailed Analysis") by Nobuhisa Kurata (August 1989), and *Seikenroku* in *Sakuma Shōzan, Yokoi Shōnan*, ed. Rei Matsuura (Chuo Koronsha, June 1984).

As with Hashimoto Sanai's *Keihatsuroku* ("Treatise on Enlightenment") and Yoshida Shoin's *Ryūkonroku* ("Soulful Minute"), I first read the original text of Shozan's *Seikenroku* with Japanese readings to ascertain the meaning. I would then have produced a literal translation, but there are already many such translations in existence. And although these differ from each other in various minor details, there are currently more similarities than differences between them. Therefore, the base text for this publication was taken from the version edited by Shinano Kyoiku Kai (Ref. 1 in the bibliography). The literal translation was based on the Nihon Shiso Taikei 55 version (Ref. 9), with consideration for the convenience of readers in English and non-specialist readers in Japanese.

Many liberal translations have also been published with commentaries. Here, I have endeavoured to provide the original text, literal translation, free translation and English translation side by side for reference by readers. I would take this opportunity to express my heartfelt gratitude for the efforts of my predecessors.

For various historical reasons, the pseudonym "Shozan" is sometimes rendered as "Zozan" in Japanese. Except in certain specific cases, however, the name is uniformly spelt "Shozan" in this publication, based on the article *Sakuma Shōzan – Gagō Koshō no Kimete* ("Sakuma Shozan: Reasons for Deciding Pseudonyms") in the Journal of the Faculty of Liberal Arts and Science, Shinshu University (see Ref. 78). To stimulate interest among non-Japanese readers who know nothing of Sakuma Shozan, and particularly those in the English-speaking world, I have endeavoured to add visual appeal by including a relatively large number of images connected with Sakuma Shozan, such as books and letters, manuscripts in his own hand, letters of opinion, calligraphic works, picture scrolls and rarely seen diagrams. The sources for these are given at the end of the book and at various points in the text. Although individual credits are not given on each page, the main image sources are *Sakuma Shōzan no Sekai* ("The World of Sakuma Shozan") courtesy of the Sanada Treasure Museum Zozan Memorial Hall, *Sakuma Shōzan to Zōzan Jinja* ("Sakuma Shozan and Zozan Shrine"), *Matsushiro Han to Kurofune Raikō* ("The Matsushiro Domain and the Perry Expedition"), and *Sanada-ke no Kagaku Gijutsu* ("Science and Technology of the Sanada Family"). I would here like to express my profound gratitude for permission to use these images.

自然科学(流体力学、流体工学、流体機械)を専門とする筆者の余技とはいえ、本書の英訳を志して7年が経過した。『啓発録』英訳の試みからは合計22年が経った。

　今回はからずも幕末維新期という日本歴史の断面において、橋本左内の『啓発録』、吉田松陰の『留魂録』、佐久間象山の『省諐録』という、いわば幕末三部作を曲がりなりにも完成させることができ、肩の荷をおろした感がある。

　乱暴な回顧が許されるとしたら、この幕末三部作英訳を終え、筆者は「橋本左内は例えば井伊直弼が最も恐れたほどの不世出の天才的政治家、吉田松陰はペリー黒船に飛び乗ったほどの胆略最高の至誠的教育者、佐久間象山は国力を高めるため西洋技術を本気で移植しようとした最右翼の理系的思想家であった」＿＿と愚考している。

　最後に『省諐録』の英訳に対し、英国在住のAndrew DRIVER氏の校閲と多大な添削を戴きました。DRIVER氏は英国Oxford大学・比較言語学Diploma課程修了、英国作家団体(The Society of Authors)、翻訳者協会(Translators' Association)、英国公認言語学会(Chartered Institute of Linguists)の正会員で現在まで多くの翻訳著作物を発刊しているプロの翻訳家です。ここに長期間にわたる質疑応答、及び図表類の翻訳作業をふくめ献身的な協力を賜りました。この場を借りて心より感謝いたします。

　また佐久間象山に関連する諸研究調査上、特に信濃国松代における藩の豪商であった八田家の第11代当主・八田慎蔵氏に大変お世話になりました。八田家は第六代・八田慎蔵氏(文政十二年生まれ)を中心に代々藩の御勝手御用役被仰付きを務め、佐久間象山と長年直接接触したため、本書でも図示した象山直筆の『水墨山水画』や各種の直筆書簡巻物の実物を拝見させて戴き、その上貴重なお話を伺うことが出来ました。ここに篤くお礼申し上げます。また松代市の象山研究家・佐久間方三氏からは約六百首ある象山の漢詩について、その代表的なものを克明に分析したレポート(一連の・ながの市誌研究)の解説を賜り、大きな学びとなり、心より謝意を表します。

As far as I have discovered in researching this publication, no other English translation of *Seikenroku* has ever been published. Within the scope of information searched, Charles Terry published a Master's thesis titled "Sakuma Shōzan and His *Seiken-roku*" at Columbia University (USA) in 1957. An abridged version can be found in *Sources of Japanese Tradition* (Columbia University Press 2005, pp.633-638). There, extracts from *Seikenroku* are used to introduce Shozan's thought, but there is no complete translation. I was informed of this by Wolfgang Schamoni, Emeritus Professor and Doctor of Literature at the University of Heidelberg in Germany, and formerly Director of its Institute for Japanese Studies. My thanks go to Prof. Dr Schamoni for this reference material.

As a specialist in natural sciences (fluid dynamics, fluid engineering and fluid machinery), this work has been something of a hobby for me. Even so, I have spent seven full years working towards this English translation; altogether, 22 years have passed since I first attempted "Treatise on Enlightenment". Having now finally completed this "Bakumatsu triptych" of works from a cross-section of Japanese history between the Bakumatsu period and the Meiji Restoration – namely, "Treatise on Enlightenment" by Hashimoto Sanai, "Soulful Minute" by Yoshida Shoin, and "Record of Conscience" by Sakuma Shozan, I feel as though a weight has been lifted from my shoulders.

To summarize somewhat crudely, now that the English translation of this "Bakumatsu triptych" is at last complete, I am left with the impression of Hashimoto Sanai as a politician of extraordinary genius who was most feared by Ii Naosuke, for example; Yoshida Shoin as an educator of the highest integrity and great audacity, who was bold enough to board Perry's Black Ships; and Sakuma Shozan as a supreme scientific thinker, who earnestly tried to transplant western technology for the furtherance of his own country's interests.

This English translation of *Seikenroku* has been reviewed and edited by Andrew Driver in the United Kingdom. Mr Driver studied for a Diploma in Comparative Philology at Oxford University, and is a member of the Society of Authors, the Translators' Association, and the Chartered Institute of Linguists in the UK. He is a professional translator of Japanese with many published translations to his name. I would like to take this opportunity to thank Mr Driver for his help with this publication, including editorial correspondence with myself over many months, as well as his translation of picture captions and other parts of this book.

Also, in my various research on Sakuma Shozan, I received particularly notable assistance from Mr Shinzo Hatta, 11th head of the Hatta family, historically known as wealthy merchants of Matsushiro in

最末尾となりましたが、筆者の畏友であり、武士道、特に我国における日本近世史並びに武家社会論研究の第一人者である人間文化研究機構・国際日本文化研究センターの笠谷和比古教授・京都大学文学博士(2015年4月より現在同センター名誉教授、手塚山大学文学部教授)にご懇篤なる批評を頂戴しました。ここに長年にわたるご厚意に篤くお礼申し上げます。

紺野大介

the Province of Shinano. After the 6th Hatta Shinzo (born in 1829), successive generations of the Hatta family served as official purveyors of goods to the Matsushiro Domain, and had direct contact with Sakuma Shozan for many years. As a result, Mr Hatta kindly showed me the originals of *Suiboku Sansuiga* (ink landscape paintings) and various other letters and scrolls produced by Shozan in person, which I have included in this publication, as well as some precious stories. For this I offer my unreserved thanks. Also, Mr Hosan Sakuma provided commentaries on reports (a series of Nagoya city archive studies) giving in-depth analysis on some representative examples of approximately 600 Chinese poems written by Shozan. These were extremely informative, and for this I am very grateful.

As mentioned earlier, the name "Shozan" (not Zozan) has been used uniformly in this publication, based on evidence in Hiroshi Takahashi's article (see Ref. 78), among others. "Zozan" is only used in certain cases where it has become established as part of a proper noun (as in "Zozan Shrine").

Finally, I received kind criticism from my esteemed friend, Professor Kazuhiko Kasaya of the International Research Center for Japanese Studies in the National Institutes for the Humanities, and Doctor of Literature at Kyoto University (since April 2015, Emeritus Professor at the Center and Professor in the Faculty of Letters at Tezukayama University). He is the foremost researcher on Bushidō, with particular reference to the history of Japan's Premodern period and samurai society. I offer my sincere thanks to him for his kind assistance.

at Tsukushino, Tokyo

Daisuke Konno

序章

Overview of Sakuma Shozan

佐久間象山と当時の周辺事情を理解するための材料
Materials, due to understanding of Sakuma Shozan with his circumference at that time

- Letter（手紙）
- Epistle（書簡）
- Poetry（詩歌）
- Scroll（巻物）
- Diploma（免状）
- Drawing（図画）
- Painting（書画）
- Photograph（写真）
- Gravestone（石碑）

図.1 塚原卜伝免許状（象山神社）
象山17歳、父である佐久間一学から国忠（象山）に与えられた免許状。この時、既に
卜伝流を体得していたことがわかる。これは松代藩に伝承した剣術等の系統の一つで、
松代藩の足軽階層に伝えられた。

Fig. 1 Tsukahara Bokuden swordsman's licence (Zozan Shrine)
A licence given to Kunitada (Shozan) by his father Sakuma Ichigaku when Shozan was 17 years old. This proves that Shozan had already mastered the Bokuden style by that time. This style of swordsmanship had been passed down through the Matsushiro Domain and was taught to the domain's infantry class.

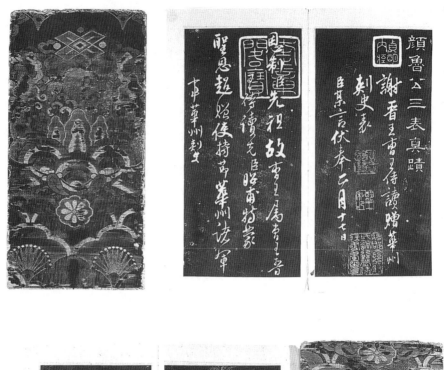

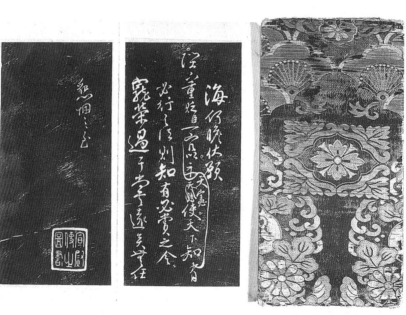

図.2 顔魯公三表帖
顔真卿の書についての石刷の手本。象山の手沢本。

Fig. 2 *Ganrokō Sanbyōchō* (*Yan Lugong San Biao Tie*)
A lithographic sampler of a work by Chinese calligrapher Yan Zhenqing. A favourite book of Shozan's.

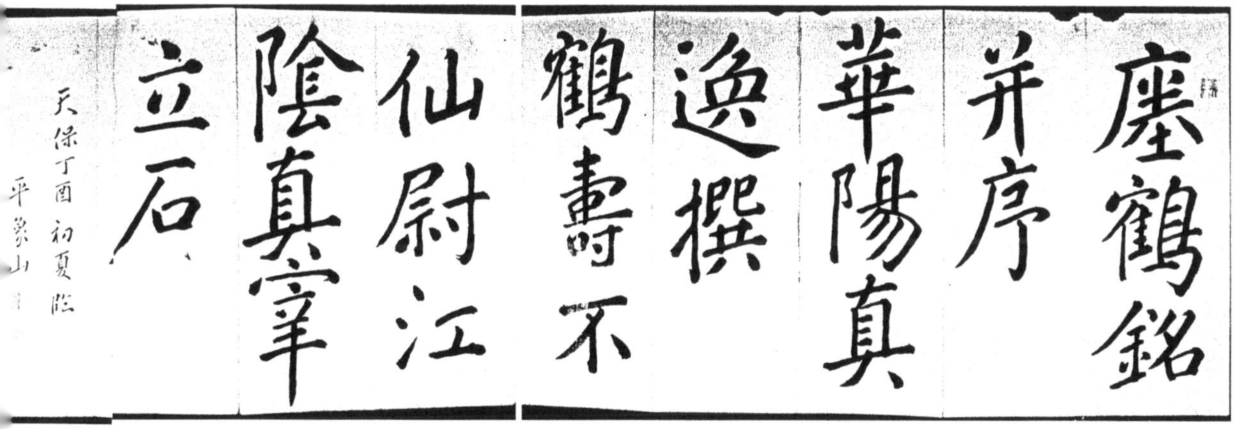

瘞鶴銘并序
華陽真逸撰
鶴壽不
仙尉江陰真宰
立石
天保丁酉初夏臨
平象山

図.3 象山26歳の書『臨瘞鶴銘并序』

奥書に「天保丁酉初夏臨」とあるので天保八年（1837年）、象山26歳時の臨書である
佐久間象山は中国唐代屈指の書家である顔真卿（709〜785）の書を絶賛している。
顔真卿は「蔵鋒」の技法の確立をし、力強さと穏やかさを兼備した独特の楷書が特徴。
象山はこの書法中に、無限の姿勢と無限の精神があるとして書を学ぶ態度に傾倒した。「瘞鶴銘」（えいかくめい）は中国・鎮江の長江中の焦山の崖に、梁代・514年（?）に刻まれたと云われている。

Fig. 3 *Eikakumei Heijo ni Nozomu* ("Contemplation on Yihe Ming and its Preface"), written by Shozan at age 26

The date inscription on the left reveals that this book is from 1837, when Shozan was 26 years old. In it, he praises a work by renowned Tang Chinese calligrapher Yan Zhenqing (709-785). Yan Zhenqing established the *zang feng* style, characterized by a unique *kai* (regular) script combining both strength and gentleness. Shozan committed himself to studying this work, as he believed the writing style embodied infinite attitude and endless spirit. "*Eikakumei*" is the Japanese reading of 瘞鶴銘 (Yihe Ming), an inscription carved on a cliff face at Jiaoshan beside the Yangtze in Zhenjiang, China. It is said to date from around 514 AD, during the Liang Dynasty.

図.4 真田幸貫画像(1791～1852)
江戸幕府第八代将軍・徳川吉宗の孫で陸奥白河藩三代藩主であった老中松平定信の次男である幸貫が養子となり、真田家第八代藩主を継いだ。天保12年(1841年)6月に幕府老中に就任、海防掛(現在の防衛大臣)となり、同年12月に侍従に昇進している。

Fig. 4 Portrait of Sanada Yukitsura (1791-1852)
Sanada Yukitsura was the second son of the Senior Councillor Matsudaira Sadanobu, who was the grandson of the 8th Edo Shogun Tokugawa Yoshimune and Head of the Mutsu Shirakawa Domain. Yukitsura was adopted into the Sanada family and became the 8th Domain Head. He was himself appointed Senior Councillor in June 1841, became Minister for Coastal Defence, and was promoted to Grand Chamberlain of Japan in December of that year.

図.5 真田幸貫公筆『磊々落々』
　　　佐久間象山跋文

『磊々落々』(らいらいらくらく)とは、度量が大きく、志が高いことを云う。下部に佐久間象山の跋文がしるされている。学問・武芸を奨励した幸貫に見いだされた象山は、この上ない後ろ盾をえて江戸へ遊学した。

Fig. 5
"*Rairai Rakuraku*" scroll by Sanada Yukitsura, with a dedication by Sakuma Shozan

"*Rairai Rakuraku*" means "Magnanimity and high aspirations". Beneath the inscription is a dedication written by Shozan. Discovered by Yukitsura, who encouraged him in learning and martial arts, Shozan went to study at Edo with his complete support.

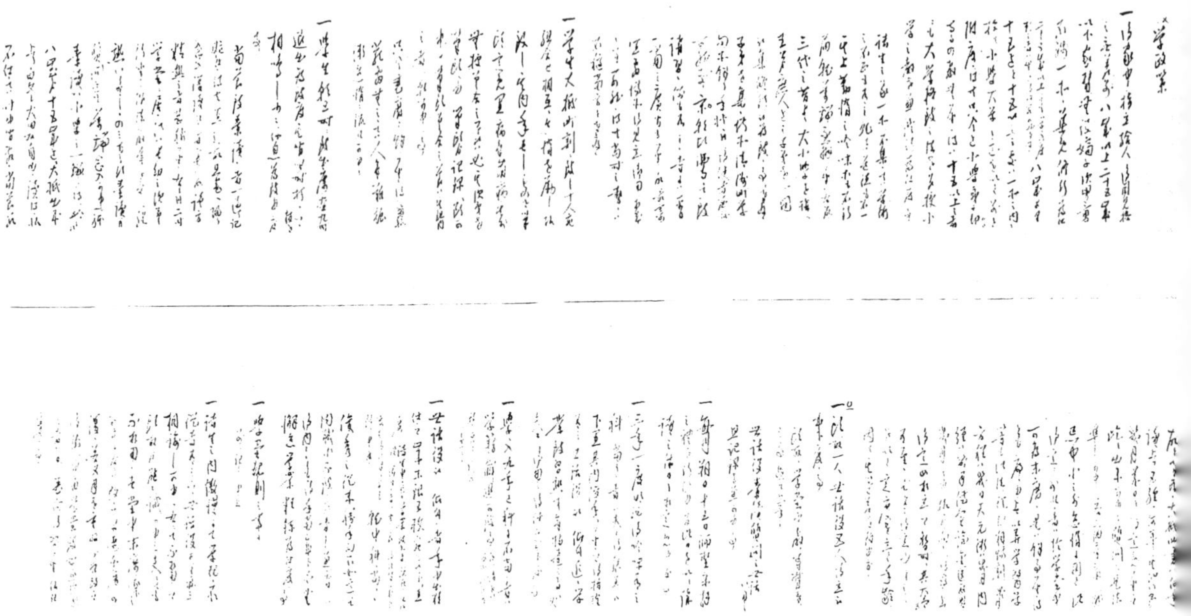

図.6 学政意見書（矢沢家文書）
象山が江戸から戻ってきた天保八年(1837)に藩へ出した意見書。藩の隆盛には学問が不可欠との見地から、建物（というハード）よりも学政（というソフト）の整備を指摘している。

Fig. 6 Opinion on academic policy (Yazawa Family archives)
A statement of opinion produced by Shozan on his return from Edo in 1837. Taking the position that academic learning would be essential for the domain to prosper, he urges the "soft approach" of prioritizing academic policy over buildings.

図.7 海防八策

天保十三年(1842) 11月、佐久間象山が藩主・真田幸貫に上申した海防論。大砲を備えるべきであることや、戦艦を建造することなど海防のために為すべき八ヶ条、並びにそれらに関する 様々な状況について述べている。幸貫の文書箱(No.18)の中から発見されたとされ、大正年間に4巻に表装された。序文は、明治・大正時代の法制学者・細川潤次郎(号・十洲)、跋文は象山の研究者であった宮本仲が記している。

Fig. 7 *Kaibō Hassaku* ("Eight Measures for Naval Defence")
A proposal for naval defence submitted by Sakuma Shozan to the Domain Head Sanada Yukitsura in November 1842. In it, he describes eight measures that should be implemented for naval defence, such as installing cannons and building warships, as well as the various situations of each. It is said to have been found in Yukitsura's document box (No.18), and was bound in four volumes during the Taisho period (1912-1925). The introduction is written by the Meiji and Taisho legal scholar Hosokawa Junjiro (pseudonym Jushu) and the dedication by Chu Miyamoto, a Sakuma Shozan researcher.

 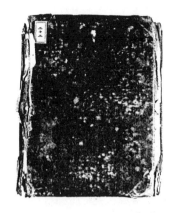

図.8 佐久間象山が手に入れ読んだとされる洋書の一部

『東洋の道徳、西洋の芸術(技術)』の名言の下、象山は西洋の科学技術書、たとえばベウセル(W.F.Beuscher)の砲術書、カステレイン(P.J.Kasteleijin)の化学書、ソンメル(J.G.Sommer)の窮理書、ショメル(M.N.Chomel)の百科事典などを入手し、読んだとされている。黒田良安からオランダ語の教授を受け、特に蟄居中に和訳されたものも含め読み、旺盛にモノつくりに取り組んだ。尚『ズーフ・ハルマ』とは、長崎のオランダ商館長 Hendrik Doeff(ズーフ)が1803〜17年間在任した折、長崎通事らの協力を得て完成したもの。ハルマとはオランダのフランソワ＝ハルマ刊行の『蘭仏辞書』を基にして作られた『蘭和辞書』のことで1833年完成。象山は国防上の観点からこれを増訂・出版を企画した。これとは別に1796年30部出版された稲村三伯による『浪留麻和解』がある。

Fig. 8 Some of the western books obtained and read by Shozan
True to his famous aphorism "Eastern ethics, Western technical learning", Shozan is said to have obtained and read many western books on science and technology. These include a gunnery manual by W.F.Beuscher, a book on chemistry by P.J.Kasteleijn, a book on physics by J.G.Sommer, and an encyclopaedia by M.N.Chomel. He received lessons in Dutch from Kurokawa Ryoan, and particularly during his house arrest, read these books (including some translated into Japanese). This inspired him to invest much effort in making mechanical devices. One of his reference works was the "Doeff-Halma" dictionary, completed by Hendrik Doeff during his tenure as Dutch Trade Commissioner at Nagasaki from 1803-17, with the assistance of Nagasaki interpreters and others. "Halma" refers to the fact that the dictionary was modelled on a Dutch-French dictionary published by the Dutchman Francois Halma and completed in 1833. Shozan planned to publish a revised and enlarged edition from the perspective of national defence. Another reference work was *Haruma Wakai* ("Halma Japanese Dictionary") by Inamura Sanpaku, of which thirty copies were published in 1796.

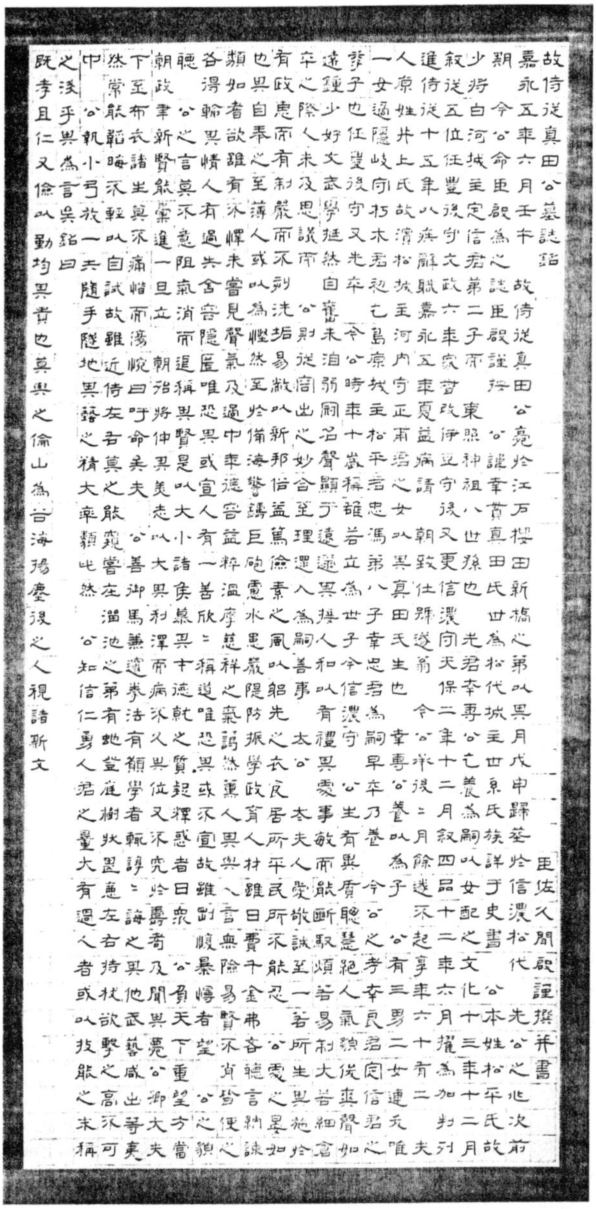

図.9 真田幸貫公墓誌銘
第八代松代藩主・真田幸貫は嘉永五年(1852)に没した。ここには幸貫が質素倹約に務め、海の警備をし、大砲を鋳造したことなどが書かれている。墓誌銘の執筆者に選ばれた象山はその績を称賛している。尚、象山が書き上げた草稿係の役人が人に籠字で模写させ、原書を秘匿これを聞いた象山が奪い返し、真田家へ納めたもので原本も現存している。象山41歳時の拓

Fig. 9 Sanada Yukitsura's epitaph
Sanada Yukitsura, 8th Head of the Matsushiro Domain, died in 1852. His epitaph mentions his devotion to austerity, coastal protection and the manufacture of cannons, among others. Shozan, who was chosen to write the epitaph, praises these achievements. The official in charge had a copy made of Shozan's draft manuscript, and the original was hidden away as an emolument. When Shozan heard this, he stole it back and delivered it to the Sanada family, which is why it still exists today. This rubbing was made when Shozan was 41 years old.

図.10 力士雷電之碑（左に雷電為右衛門の勝川春亭画）
江戸時代後期の伝説的力士・雷電為右衛門（1767～1823）は松代の西南に位置する信濃国小県郡大石村（現在の長野県東御市）の出身。現役相撲生活21年、通算の黒星合計は僅かに10番、勝率.962で大相撲史上未曾有の最強力士とされている。真田幸貫公墓誌銘と並んで漢詩に造詣が深い佐久間象山の拓本の代表作。

Fig. 10 Monument to the wrestler Raiden (left: a picture of Raiden Tameemon by Katsukawa Shuntei)
The legendary late Edo wrestler Raiden Tameemon (1767-1823) hailed from the village of Oishi in Chiisagata-gun, Shinano Province (today's Tomi City in Nagano Prefecture), southwest of Matsushiro. Raiden is regarded as the strongest wrestler ever known in sumo history, suffering only ten losses for a win ratio of 0.962 in a career lasting 21 years. Alongside the epitaph to Sanada Yukitsura, this is a representative work of stone rubbing by Sakuma Shozan, who was deeply accomplished in Chinese poetry.

Katsu Kaishu (1823〜1899)

図.11 額「海舟書屋」(宮下劭氏寄託)

1852年(嘉永5年)に書かれた象山の書。同様のものが幾つかあるが、左に記載年代が記されており、象山が木挽町に塾を置いた翌年のもであることが明確である。象山の門弟である勝海舟が、この額の「海舟」の文字を自分の号とした。

Fig. 11 "*Kaishū Sho-oku*" plaque (by kind permission of Mr Tsutomu Miyashita)
Brush-written by Shozan in 1852. There are several similar plaques, but the dating on the left proves that this one was produced in the year after Shozan set up his school in Kobiki-cho. Shozan's pupil Katsu Kaishu took the first two characters of this plaque (海舟, "Kaishū") as his pseudonym.

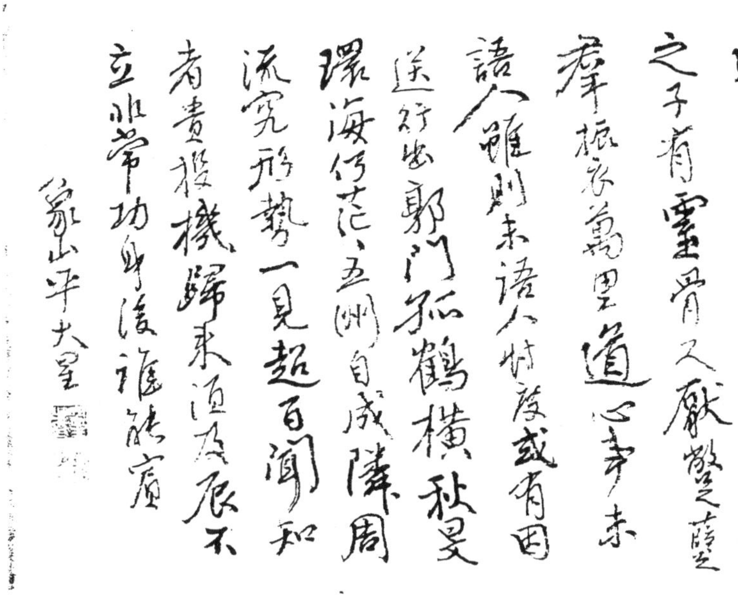

送義卿
之子有霊骨又厭蟄之藝
奮振家萬里道心事未
語人雖則未語人忖度或有因
送行出郭門孤鶴横秋旻
環海信茫五洲自成隣周
流究形勢一見超百聞知
者貴投機歸來須及辰不
立非常功身後誰能賓
象山平大星

義卿を送る
之の子霊骨あり、久しく蟄蟄の群を厭う。
衣を奮う万里の道、心事未だ
則ち未だ人に語げずと雖も、忖度或は因るあり。
行くを送って郭門を出ずれば、孤鶴秋旻に横たわる。
環海何ぞ茫々たる、五州自ら隣を為す。
周流形勢を究めよ、一見は百聞に超ゆ。
智者は機に投ずるを貴び、帰来須らく辰に及ぶべし。
非常の功を立てずんば、身後誰れか能く賓せん。

象山平大星

図.12 吉田義卿を送る詩（宮下劭氏寄託）
象山の門弟、吉田松陰は外国の見聞を希求し、長崎に向かい停泊と聞いていたロシア船に乗り込む決意をした。象山は松陰のこの時の気持ちに応えるべく詩をかいた。また餞別として4両を渡した。

Fig. 12 Farewell poem to Yoshida Shoin (by kind permission of Mr Tsutomu Miyashita)
Shozan's pupil Yoshida Shoin was determined to go to Nagasaki and board a Russian ship, where he hoped to learn the ways of foreign countries. Shozan wrote this poem in support of Shoin's aspirations at the time. He also gave him 4 *ryō* (a sum of money) as a parting gift.

松陰先生が最初に到達したる「ミシシピー」号

松陰先生が最後に到達したる彼理坐乗の旗艦「ボーハタン」号甲板上日本人饗応の図

図.13 吉田松陰とペリー黒船

(徳富猪一郎著『吉田松陰』東京民友社刊 p.181 より)

神奈川県下田。安政元年1854年3月27日、著書の表現によれば上図は松陰が最初に到達したミシシッピー号、下図は松陰が最後に到達したペリー乗船の旗艦ボーハタン号。吉田松陰と金子重之助による甲板上の饗応、密航渡海事件の様子。文献30.及び北京大学の王暁秋教授によれば、この時、2名はペリー艦隊の主席通訳官S.W.ウイリアムズとの間の漢文(中国語)や日本語の会話が上手く通じず、松陰は中国人漢文通訳・羅森との会話を求めた。しかし松陰と羅森の二人の会話が日米関係に影響を及ぼすことを怖れたウイリアムズは「羅森は就寝中」＿＿＿として逢せなかったため、松陰・重之助の密航は不首尾に終ったとされている。(文献.30 及び 107,108)

Fig. 13 Yoshida Shoin and Perry's Black Ships
(from Iichiro Tokutomi, *Yoshida Shōin*, Tokyo Minyusha, p.181)
Shimoda, Kanagawa Prefecture, March 27, 1854. According to the captions in the book, the top picture shows the US Steam Frigate Mississippi, which Shoin reached first, and the bottom picture Perry's own flagship the Powhatan, which he reached last. The latter picture shows the banquet being given by Yoshida Shoin and Kaneko Shigenosuke on the deck, the scene of the stowaway incident. According to Professor Wang Xiaoqiu of Peking University, the two Japanese were unable to converse properly in Chinese or Japanese with S.W.Williams, the Chief Interpreter for the Perry fleet, and so Shoin asked to speak with the Chinese interpreter Luo Sen. However, fearing that a conversation between Shoin and Luo Sen could have an adverse impact on Japan-US relations, Williams told him that Luo Sen was asleep and thus prevented the meeting. This is said to be why the stowaway attempt by Shoin and others ended in failure (see Refs. 30 107 and 108).

図.14 佐久間象山門下の『二虎』
　　　佐久間象山が最も期待していた弟子二人。
象山は「義卿（吉田松陰）の胆略、炳文（小林虎三郎）の学識、希世の才」と絶賛。象山門下で「二虎」と呼ばれた。小林虎三郎（字は炳文、号は病翁）は幼少時に疱瘡により左目を失明。1850年江戸留学し象山門下となった。『興学私議』を著す。戊辰戦争で壊滅的な打撃を受けた長岡で、長岡藩の支藩である三根山藩が窮状を察し『米百表』の寄贈を受けた。しかし長岡藩の大参事・虎三郎は「百俵の米も食えばたちまち無くなるが、教育にあてれば明日の一万、百万俵になる」とし配給を待ち望む藩士に忍耐させ、寺の本堂を仮校舎として国漢学校を開校させた。この逸話は山本有三の戯曲にもなった。
　　因みに、仏国人ダゲールによる銀板写真の発明は1839年、米国の写真商人フリーマンが横浜で我国最初の写真館を開いたのが1860年、従って1859年に『安政の大獄』で斬刑に処せられた吉田松陰や橋本左内の実写真は無い。上図左方の吉田松陰(1830〜1859)は日本画家・前田青邨の「蓮台寺の松陰」よりのスケッチ。小林虎三郎(1828〜1877)は写真。

Fig. 14 "Two tigers" under Sakuma Shozan
Two followers of whom Sakuma Shozan had the highest expectations. Shozan praised them as having "the courage and wit of Gikyo (Yoshida Shoin), the erudition of Heibun (Kobayashi Torasaburo), and rare talent". They were known as the "two tigers" among Shozan's followers. Kobayashi Torasaburo (courtesy name Heibun, pseudonym Heio) had lost his left eye after contracting smallpox in childhood. He went to study at Edo in 1850 and entered Shozan's tutelage. He wrote *Kogaku Shigi* ("Personal View on the Promotion of Learning"). After his Nagaoka Domain had suffered great destruction in the Boshin War, the Mineyama Clan (a branch of the Nagaoka Domain) sympathized with its plight and made a donation of "100 bags of rice". But Torasaburo, as a leading official of the Nagaoka Domain, said "If these hundred bags of rice are eaten, they will be lost instantly, but if they are put towards education, they will become the ten thousand or one million bags of tomorrow." The clansmen who were looking forward to their food supplies were thus persuaded to persevere. The rice was sold and the proceeds used to fund the opening of the Kokkan Gakko school, set up in the main hall of a temple as a temporary schoolroom. This episode has been immortalized in a play by Yuzo Yamamoto. Incidentally, the silver plate photographic process was invented by Frenchman Louis-Jacques-Mandé Daguerre in 1839, but it was not until 1860 that Japan's first photographic studio was opened in Yokohama by the American professional photographer Orrin Freeman. As a result, there are no photographic portraits of Yoshida Shoin or Hashimoto Sanai, who were sentenced to death in 1859 as part of the "Ansei Purge". The picture of Yoshida Shoin (1830-1859), on the left above, is a sketch from "Shoin at Rendai-ji Temple" by the Japanese artist Seison Maeda. The picture of Kobayashi Torasaburo (1828-1877) is a real-life portrait.

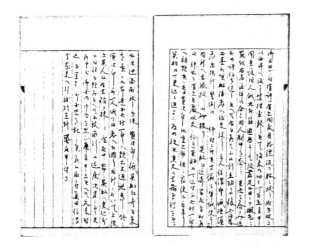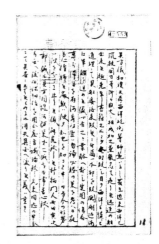

図.15 佐久間象山・蟄居申渡状（京都大学付属図書館）
門弟・吉田松陰の渡海密航事件は、佐久間象山が深く係わっていると判断した幕府は、象山に対し蟄居を申し渡した。

Fig. 15 Warrant for house arrest of Sakuma Shozan (Kyoto University Library)
The Tokugawa shogunate judged Sakuma Shozan to be heavily complicit in Yoshida Shoin's stowaway attempt and sentenced him to house arrest.

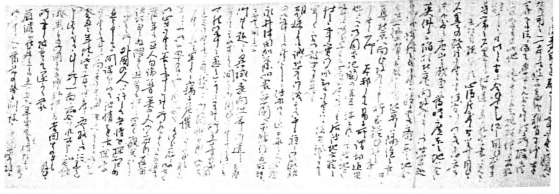

図.16 佐久間象山書簡（象山神社）
象山が勝海舟に宛てた書簡。アメリカなどとの条約締結にふれ松陰の渡航失敗に関連させ、今後の世界との関わりについて危惧している。

Fig. 16 Letter written by Sakuma Shozan (Zozan Shrine)
A letter addressed to Katsu Kaishu. Mentions the signing of treaties with the USA and others, linking them to Shoin's failed stowaway attempt. The letter also expresses misgivings over future relations with the outside world.

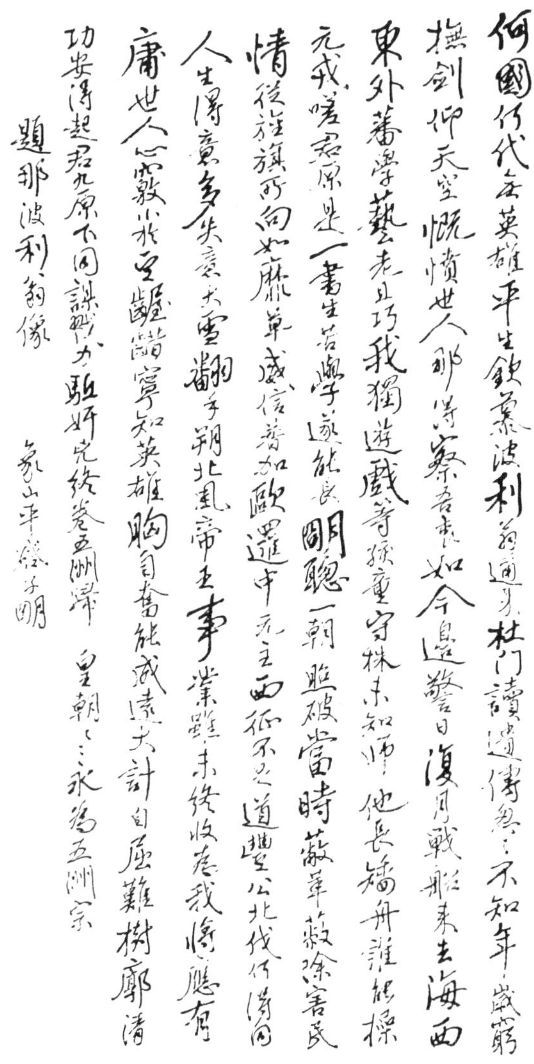

図.17 題那波利翁像詩（京都大学付属図書館）
象山が蟄居した1854年（安政元年）頃の作品。英雄ナポレオンの伝記を読み、その感想・感激を詠んだもの。ヨーロッパを征したナポレオンの行動力に学ぶべきである、との自説を述べている。

Fig. 17 *Dai Naporeon Zōshi* ("Eulogy for Napoleon", Kyoto University Library)

A work by Shozan from around 1854, when he was put under house arrest. It records his impressions and emotions on reading Napoleon's biography. Shozan also states his personal opinion that lessons should be learnt from Napoleon's positive dynamism in conquering Europe.

図.18 ペリー肖像(1794〜1858)
『日本遠征石版画集』ウィルヘルム・ハイネ
（神奈川県立博物館）
日本遠征を終え帰国後に撮影した銀板写真を基に作成された石版画。

Fig. 18 Portrait of Commodore Perry (1794-1858) From "Graphic Scenes in the Japan Expedition" by Wilhelm Heine (Kanagawa Prefectural Library)
Lithograph based on a daguerreotype taken after Perry's return from the Japan expedition.

図.19 ペリー艦隊の日本までの航路
蒸気船の航海には途中で石炭の補給が不可欠であった。そのためペリー艦隊は、アメリカを出港すると大西洋を横断し、石炭補給基地のあるアフリカの西海岸を南下してインド洋に入り、更にシンガポールを経て香港、上海に至る航路を進んだ。上海から琉球王国の那覇に寄港し、ここで最終の艦隊を編成し、日本へ向かった。

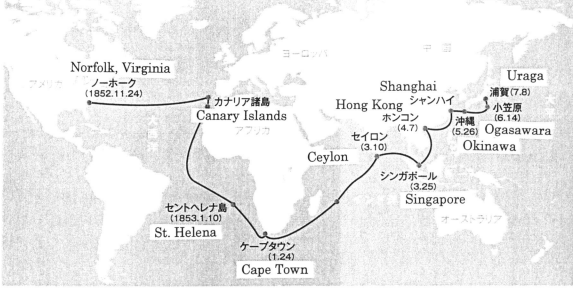

Fig. 19 The route taken by Perry's expedition to Japan
Navigation by steamship depended on stops for refuelling with coal along the way. So after leaving America, Perry's expedition first crossed the Atlantic, then travelled southwards down the west coast of Africa, where there were coal refuelling bases. From there, the expedition rounded the Cape to enter the Indian Ocean, then took a course via Singapore to Hong Kong and Shanghai. After Shanghai, it made a stop at Naha in the Ryukyu Kingdom, where a final fleet was formed for the journey to Japan.

1866年のニューヨーク海軍軍港
サスケハナ号の姿もある（中央）(U.S. Naval Historical Center 所蔵)

ペリー艦隊旗艦・
サスケハナ号
（幕末・明治・大正 回顧
80年史 東洋文化協會）

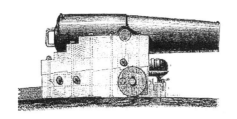

ペリー艦隊のミシシッピー号
に搭載されていたペクサン砲
〔仏製〕

ペリー艦隊のサスケハナ号に
搭載されていたダールグレ
ン砲〔米製〕（写真：www.
news.navy.mil より）

ペリー艦隊のサスケハナ号に
搭載されていたパロット砲
〔米製〕（写真：cs.finescale.
com より）

図.20 ペリー艦隊の蒸気外輪フリゲート艦サスケハナ号及
びミシシッピー号と各種砲。
（出典：US navy web site より。引用は文献60より）

Fig. 20 The US Steam Frigates Susquehanna and Mississippi from the Perry expedition, and various cannons (Source: Internet web site from US Navy; Cited Bibliography 60)

図.21. 中国人通訳「羅森」

（大日本古文書・幕末外国関係文書）

中国・広東出身の士大夫で号は向喬。科挙に及第しても官職につかず官民の間をとりもった知識階層の人。1854年ペリー艦隊二度目の来航の際、主席通訳官S.W.ウイリアムズに同行し漢文通訳を務めた。ウイリアムズの通訳があまり機能せず、本来オランダ語が基本であったが日米談判は漢文（中国語）が用いられた。博学で教養高い羅森の日本側の評価は極めて高く、日米和親条約の談判の全工程に参加。有能でセンス良く、幕末の日本で非常に有名な人物となった。交渉にあたった聡明な開明派幕臣・平山謙二郎らは羅森を絶賛した。（羅森の画の右上に「清朝人・羅森」が確認できる）。

Fig. 21 The Chinese interpreter Luo Sen
Source: *Bakumatsu Gaikoku Kankei Monjo* ("Historical Records of Bakumatsu Foreign Relations") in *Dai Nihon Komonjo* ("Japanese Historical Manuscripts")
A scholar-official from Canton in China, pseudonym Xiangqiao. Luo Sen was an intellectual who passed the Chinese civil service examinations but did not take public office, thus mediating between public and private. He travelled with the 2nd Perry Expedition in 1854, serving as a Chinese interpreter to accompany the Chief Interpreter S.W.Williams. Interpreting by Williams had not worked well, and although Dutch was the normal medium, Chinese was used for the Japan-US negotiations. Luo Sen was very well received by the Japanese side on account of his great erudition, and took part in the whole process of negotiation for the Japan-US Treaty of Amity and Commerce. With his professional skill and good sense, he became a noted celebrity in Bakumatsu Japan. Among others, he was praised by the knowledgeable Hirayama Kenjiro, a progressive vassal of the shogunate who was involved in the negotiations. (The inscription "Luo Sen of the Qing Dynasty" can be seen at the top right of the picture).

図.22 米艦渡来記念図
　　　堀口貞明筆　横浜開港資料館所蔵

全国に残るペリー関係の絵図は、作者や作成された時期が不明のものが多い。しかし本資料は絵巻きが作成されるまでの経緯が記され、作者である堀口貞明は、現在の群馬県藤岡市の農民で、江戸時代末期に江戸で旗本・浦上氏の用人になった人物であることが分かっている。絵巻きの絵図は、白川藩・宮津藩・鯖江藩らの藩士が描いたものから模写したことが分かる。また堀口貞明は佐久間象山や山寺常山、三村晴山といった松代藩士とも交流があった。

Fig. 22 *Beikan Tōrai Kinenzu* ("Pictorial Commemorating the Arrival of the American Ships") by Horiguchi Sadaaki (Yokohama Archives of History)
Many surviving illustrations connected with Perry are of unknown authorship and date. However, this particular scroll gives specific details of the process leading to its creation. It tells us that the artist Horiguchi Sadaaki was a farmer in what is now Fujioka City in Gumma Prefecture, and that he became a manager for the Uragami retainers toward the end of the Edo period. It also reveals that the pictures on the scroll were copied from originals drawn by samurai from the Shirakawa, Miyazu and Sabae Domains. The artist was acquainted with Matsushiro clansmen Yamadera Jozan and Mimura Seizan, as well as Sakuma Shozan.

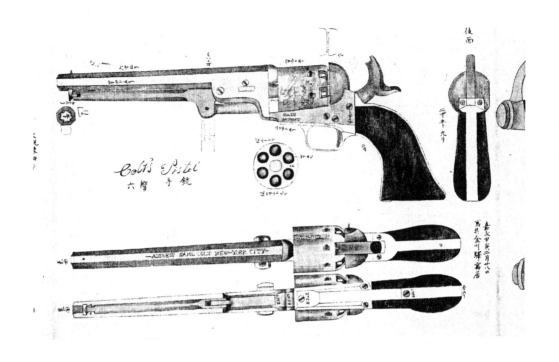

図.23 黒船来航画巻(部分)「短銃」
　　　横浜開港資料館所蔵

本資料は蒸気船やアメリカ人の様子、所持していた武器などを描いた絵巻きである。
　図藩の銃の絵は細かい部分まで詳細に描かれたおり、実際に手に取って描いたものと思われる。絵図には嘉永7年2月28日に金川（神奈川）駅にて写したものと記されている。

Fig. 23 *Kurobune Raikō Emaki* ("Picture Scroll of the Perry Expedition" / Part)
"Revolver" (Yokohama Archives of History)
This is a picture scroll depicting steamships, the appearance of the Americans, the weapons they carried, etc. The pistol in the illustration is drawn in considerable detail, suggesting that the artist actually held the pistol in his hand. The text explains that the picture was drawn at Kanagawa post station on February 28, 1854.

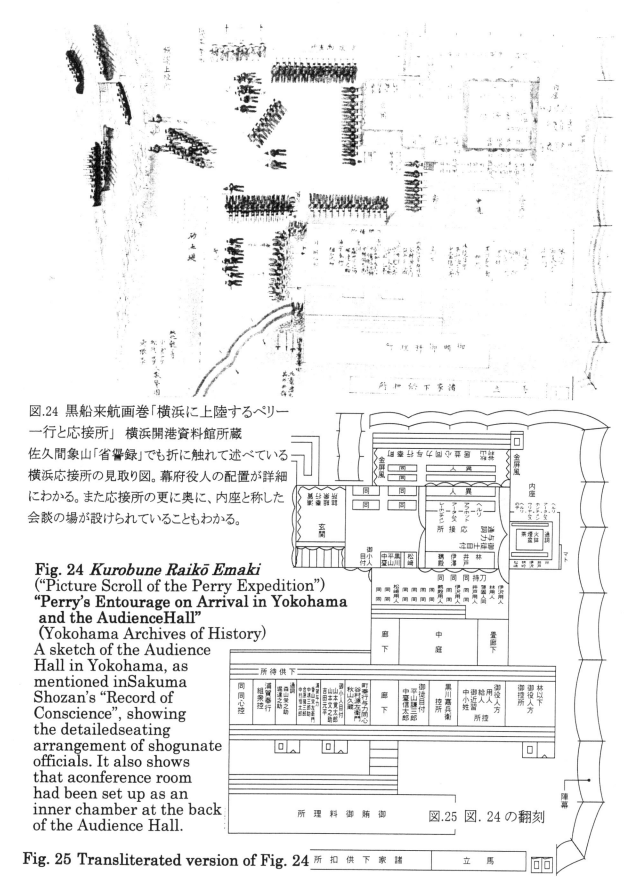

図.24 黒船来航画巻「横浜に上陸するペリー一行と応接所」 横浜開港資料館所蔵

佐久間象山「省諐録」でも折に触れて述べている横浜応接所の見取り図。幕府役人の配置が詳細にわかる。また応接所の更に奥に、内座と称した会談の場が設けられていることもわかる。

Fig. 24 *Kurobune Raikō Emaki* ("Picture Scroll of the Perry Expedition") "Perry's Entourage on Arrival in Yokohama and the AudienceHall" (Yokohama Archives of History)
A sketch of the Audience Hall in Yokohama, as mentioned inSakuma Shozan's "Record of Conscience", showing the detailedseating arrangement of shogunate officials. It also shows that aconference room had been set up as an inner chamber at the back of the Audience Hall.

図.25 図.24の翻刻

Fig. 25 Transliterated version of Fig. 24

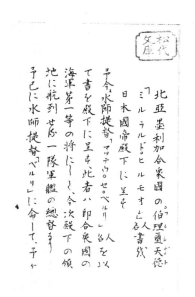
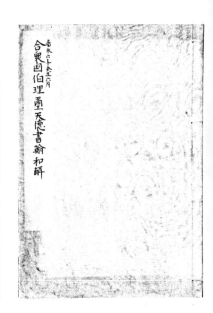

図.26 合衆国書翰和解

嘉永6年(1853)6月、幕府がペリーより受理したフィルモア米国大統領よりの親書の和解(和訳)。日米両国が親交を結び、通商や漂流民の保護、蒸気船のための石炭供給などを要求している。大統領からペリーへの全権委任状や、ペリーから日本皇帝宛ての書簡などの和訳も記されている。老中・阿部正弘はこの親書の和解の漢文版を諸大名に公開し、今後の対応について広く意見を集めたため、多くの写本が作られた。本資料もその一つと考えられる。

Fig. 26 Japanese translation of a letter from the US President
A translation of a letter from US President Fillmore, delivered to the shogunate by Perry in June 1853. It requests that both countries "should live in friendship and have commercial intercourse with each other", as well as seeking protection for shipwrecked Americans and supplies of coal for steamships, among others. There are also Japanese translations of the President's commission conferring the power of plenipotentiary on Perry, and letters from Perry to the Emperor of Japan. The Senior Councillor Masahiro Abe distributed a classical Chinese prose version of this translation to the *daimyo* feudal lords and broadly canvassed their opinions on what do to next. As a result, many copies were made. This is thought to be one of them.

図.27 横浜応接秘図　個人所蔵
幕府儒官の林家に伝来されたとする絵図。「神奈川公役日記」（東北大学附属図書館）によると高川文筌は林復斎の求めに応じて絵図を献上している。

Fig. 27 *Yokohama Ōsetsu Hizu* ("Secret Illustration of the Reception at Yokohama") (privately owned)
An illustration thought to have been kept by the Hayashi family, official teachers of Confucianism to the shogunate. According to the *Kanagawa Kōeki Nikki* ("Kanagawa Public Service Journal", Tohoku University Library), the illustration was presented by Takakawa Bunsen upon request by Hayashi Fukusai.

図.28 参考：贈り物引き渡し図
　　　（栄光教育文化研究所出版『ペリー艦隊日本遠征記』）

嘉永七年(1854)2月15日には米国から、蒸気機関車の模型も送られ、横浜応接所の裏地へレールも引かれ、蒸気機関車が組み立てられ、アメリカ人技師によって運転が行われた。当時の日本人にとって米国の献上物の中で、ひときわ目を引くものであった模様である。

Fig. 28 Reference: "Delivery of American Presents at Yokohama" (from *Perry Kantai Nippon Enseiki*, "Journal of the Expedition of the Perry Fleet to Japan", published by Eiko Educational Culture Institute)
On February 15, 1854, a miniature steam locomotive was sent from the USA. Rails were laid to the back of the Audience Hall at Yokohama, and the locomotive was assembled and operated by American engineers. Of all the gifts presented by the Americans, this seems to have attracted particular interest among the Japanese of the time.

図.29 米国使節彼里(ペリー)提督来朝図絵(部分)
「幕府、米使への贈り物運搬に力士を使う」
嘉永7年(1854)2月26日、幕府よりペリー一行へ答礼品が贈られた。贈り物の一つ、米俵の運搬に江戸の力士93人に運ばせるというパフォーマンスを行った。また同日には稽古相撲も披露された。アメリカ人は力士の弾力ある肉体に驚いていた様子である。

Fig. 29 *Beikoku Shisetsu Perry Teitoku Raichō Zue*
("Illustrations from US Commodore Perry's Visit to the Imperial Court" / Part)
"Shogunate uses wrestlers to carry gifts to the American envoy"
On February 26, 1854, the shogunate reciprocated by sending gifts to Perry's entourage. One of the gifts included a performance by 93 sumo wrestlers from Edo carrying rice bales. There was also a display of sumo practice that day. The Americans seem to have been amazed at the flexibility of the wrestlers' bodies.

図.30 亜米利加蒸気船と力士力競
　　　個人所蔵(長野市立博物館寄託)

Fig. 30 *Amerika Jōkisen to Rikishi Kurabe*
("American Steamships and a Show of Strength by Wrestlers")
Privately owned (by kind permission of Nagano City Museum)

図.31 魏源像（1794〜1856）
清の思想家.号は良図。清末の経世家でアヘン戦争を主導した　欽差大臣・林則徐の刎頸の友。新思想の提唱者として中国を「世界に目を開かせる」役割を担った当時の知識人の代表。林則徐から与えられたイギリスの『世界地理大全』を参考に編纂させた『四洲志』を基にして『海国図志』を完成させ、最終的に全100巻の大著となった。

Fig. 31 Portrait of Wei Yuan (1794-1856)

A Chinese thinker from the Qing Dynasty. His pseudonym was Liang tu. An inseparable friend of the Imperial Commissioner Lin Zexu, the late Qing statesman who led his country into the First Opium War. As an advocate of new ideas, he was representative of contemporary intellectuals who bore the role of "opening China's eyes to the world". His *Haiguo Tuzhi* ("Illustrated Treatise on the Maritime Kingdoms") was originally based on *Sizhouzhi* ("Geography of the Four Continents"), a work compiled by Lin Zexu with reference to the *Encyclopædia of Geography* by Scotsman Hugh Murray. Wei Yuan gradually expanded the "Treatise", eventually producing a massive compendium consisting of 100 volumes.

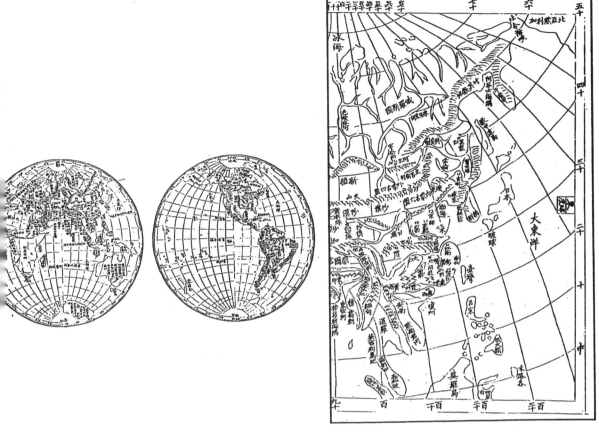

図.32 魏源『海国図志』のアジア州全図の一部
湖南省出身の清国の思想家・魏源の『海国図志』全50巻はアヘン戦争に揺れる清国よりも、日本の幕末の英傑、吉田松陰、橋本左内、佐久間象山らによって欧米列強のアジア浸食への危機感をもって真摯に詳読された。この中にはアジア全図の一部、及び日本国東界図、日本国西界図の部分に分けた表現をしている。

Fig. 32 Partial Map of Asia in Wei Yuan's *Haiguo Tuzhi*
("Illustrated Treatise on the Maritime Kingdoms")
The original 50 volumes of *Haiguo Tuzhi* ("Illustrated Treatise on the Maritime Kingdoms") by Wei Yuan, a thinker from Hunan Province in Qing Dynasty China, were of great interest to Yoshida Shoin, Hashimoto Sanai, Sakuma Shozan and other prominent figures of Bakumatsu Japan. If anything, Wei Yuan's work evoked in them a greater sense of crisis over the erosion of Asia by Western powers than it did in Qing China itself, rocked as it was by the First Opium War. The book included a partial map of Asia and maps of eastern and western Japan, as seen in contemporary expressions.

図.33 江川太郎左衛門の御礼奉申上候書付

　江川太郎左衛門(1801〜1855)は江戸後期の幕臣で伊豆韮山の代官。洋学に強い関心を示し、幕府の命もあり高島秋帆(1798〜1866)の門下生となり高島流西洋砲術を習得。佐久間象山、橋本左内、大鳥圭介、桂小五郎などは江川門下となり教示を受けた。これはNo.38 大砲の原寸絵図に付随した江川太郎左衛門英龍の礼状。図を江川家が松代藩に貸出し、その礼を受け取ったことへの江川からの礼状。象山にとっては勘定吟味役まで昇進した江川の秘密主義は人間的にそりが合わなかった。このため高島秋帆門下の砲術家で開放的な下曽根金三郎に学ぶことが多かった様子である。

Fig. 33 Letter of Acknowledgement from Egawa Tarozaemon
Egawa Tarozaemon (1801-1855) was a shogunate official in the Late Edo period and a governor of Nirayama in Izu. He exhibited a strong interest in Western learning. Partly under orders from the shogunate, he enrolled as a pupil of Takashima Shuhan (1798-1866), who taught him Takashima-style Western gunnery. In turn, Sakuma Shozan, Hashimoto Sanai, Ohtori Keisuke, Katsura Kogoro and others became his pupils and were taught by him. The picture shows a letter of acknowledgement by Egawa Tarozaemon Hidetatsu attached to the full-sized drawing of a gun shown in Fig. 38. The Egawas had loaned the drawing to the Matsushiro Domain, and Egawa thanks Shozan for the thanks received. Shozan felt that Egawa, who had risen to the position of Inspector of Accounts, had an unnatural inclination towards secrecy. He seems to have learnt more from Shimosone Kinzaburo, another pupil of Takashima Shuhan and a gunner who had a more open-minded approach.

図.34 『佐久間象山大志伝』第二巻の挿絵。
明治15年7月(1882)出版。編集人：清水義壽、出版人：市川量造、発行所：髙見甚左衛門。勝海舟が『省諐録』を出版した10年後の上梓。松代藩軍議役・佐久間象山と小倉藩軍議役・望月何某との（志士決策を論ずる）面談の様子。

尚、『省諐録』にしばしば出てくる"望月"は、望月主水のことで、松代藩家老（名は貫恕）。象山の有力な支援者であった。安政元年（1854）に松代藩が横浜警備にあたった折には、総督として象山を軍議役に任用した。また象山が密航渡海事件に連座して松代で蟄居するようになってからは、自分の別邸を象山に提供している。

Fig. 34 Illustration in *Sakuma Shōzan Taishiden* ("The Ambitions of Sakuma Shozan") Vol. 2

Published in July 1882, ed. Shimizu Yoshihisa, publ. Ichikawa Ryozo, distributed by Takami Jinzaemon. Printed ten years after the publication of *Seikenroku* by Katsu Kaishu. The illustration depicts a meeting to discuss allied strategy between Sakuma Shozan, military adviser to the Matsushiro Domain and Mochizuki Nanigashi, military adviser to the Kokura Domain.

The name "Mochizuki" appears from time to time in *Seikenroku*, where it refers to Mochizuki Mondo, chief retainer of the Matsushiro Domain (given name Kannyo) and a powerful supporter of Shozan. When the Matsushiro Domain was appointed to guard Yokohama in 1854, Mochizuki appointed Shozan a military adviser in his capacity as Governor-General. After Shozan was sentenced to house arrest in Matsushiro for complicity in Shoin's stowaway incident, he provided his own villa for use by Shozan.

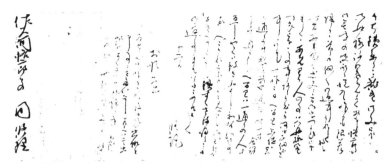

図.35 佐久間象山書簡（横浜市歴史博物館蔵）

象山が息子の格二郎と妻の順に送った書簡。嘉永7年（1854年）ペリー上陸の際、ペリーが象山に会釈した、と記されている。

Fig. 35 Letter from Sakuma Shozan (Yokohama History Museum)
A letter written by Shozan to his son Kakujiro and his wife Jun. In it, he mentions that Perry greeted him when the latter landed in 1854.

図.36 済生三方

杉田玄白の孫である蘭学者・杉田成卿の著作『済生三方』。ペリー来航の際、アメリカ大統領の国書を翻訳した。蕃書調所の教授に迎えられ「蘭語辞典」の編纂などに尽くした。名利に疎く世俗の妥協を嫌った成卿は、蘭語の門人であった橋本左内から政治的に大きな影響を受け、国家の安危にも非常な関心を示した。一方、佐久間象山は黒田良安のほか成卿にもオランダ語を習った。象山は医学を通じて成卿と昵懇な関係にあったため、出版に際しこの著作に一文を入れている。

Fig. 36 *Saisei Sanpō* ("Lifesaving Surgery")
A book on surgical procedures published by Sugita Seikei, a scholar of Dutch studies and grandson of Sugita Genpaku. He translated documents from the US President when the Perry expedition arrived in Japan. His other efforts include compiling a "Dutch dictionary" on request by a teacher at the Bansho Shirabesho (Institute for the Study of Barbarian Books, forerunner of Tokyo University). Seikei, who felt little concern for fame or profit and disliked the compromises of the secular world, was politically influenced by Hashimoto Sanai, a pupil of the Dutch language, and showed very great concern for the welfare of the nation. Sakuma Shozan learnt Dutch from Seikei as well as from Kurokawa Ryoan. He was on friendly terms with Seikei via medicine and other interests, and contributed a message to mark the publication.

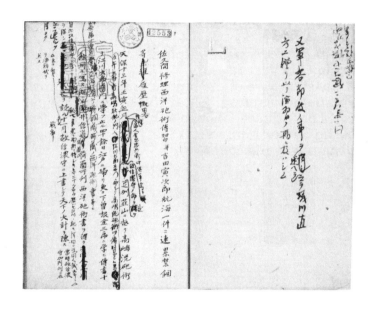

図.37 佐久間象山砲術履歴（京都大学附属図書館）
砲術家としての佐久間象山の経歴がわかる。象山の砲術実験について編年体で記述されている。北沢正誠の編になるものと思われる。

Fig. 37 Sakuma Shozan's career in gunmanship (Kyoto University Library)
This reveals details of Sakuma Shozan's history as a gunman and describes his gunnery experiments in chronological order. Thought to have been compiled by Kitazawa Masanari.

図. 38 迅発撃銃分解図
松代藩士・片井京助が安政三年（1856）に発明した元込銃についての構造を解き、その利便性について触れている。これを時の大老・井伊直弼に提出したが却下された。

Fig. 38 *Jinpatsu Gekijū Bunkaizu* ("Exploded View Drawing of a Quick-Firing Gun")
Explains the structure of the breech-loading rifle invented by the Matsushiro samurai Katai Kyosuke in 1856, and mentions its usefulness. Shozan submitted this to Ii Naosuke, the Senior Minister in the Tokugawa shogunate, but the design was rejected.

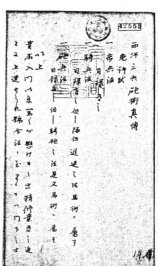

図. 39 西洋砲術真伝（京都大学附属図書館）
佐久間象山が発行した西洋砲術の真伝書。象山が門弟に対して砲術の免許状を出していたことがわかる。

Fig. 39 *Seiyō Hōjutsu Shinden* ("A True Account of Western Gunmanship", Kyoto University Library)
An authentic explanation of western gunmanship, published by Sakuma Shozan. It reveals that Shozan issued gunner's licenses to his pupils. This is a copy of one of them.

辛亥春三月二十二日
將=諸子-演=五十斤石衝天砲
於松代城西生萱村-
此邊村落皆杏林
往往有=山桃-間レ之
開花爛漫彌望如=紅雲-
而放=巨砲於其間-
眞奇景也

春野乘レ晴演=大砲-
四林桃杏正芳菲
一聲霹靂震=天地-
萬樹紅花撩亂飛

辛亥（しんがい）の春三月二十二日
諸子（ひ）を将いて五十斤（ポンドせきしょうてんほう）石衝天砲
松代城の西生萱村（いきがやむら）にて演ず
此（こ）の辺りの村落皆杏林（きょうりん）
往往（おうおう）山桃有りて之に間（まじ）る
開花爛漫弥望紅雲（びぼうこううん）の如（ごと）し
而（しこう）して巨砲其（そ）の間（かん）に放（はな）つ
真（まこと）に奇景なり

春野（しゅんや）晴に乗じて大砲を演ず
四林（しりん）の桃杏（とうきょう）正に芳菲（ほうひ）
一声（いっせい）の霹靂（へきれき）天地に震（ふる）い
万樹（ばんじゅ）の紅花（こうか）撩乱（りょうらん）として飛ぶ

図. 40 ＜象山砲術試射地＞碑 （千曲市生萱）
嘉永四年（1851）の春、佐久間象山は松代藩領の生萱で、大砲の試射を実施した。碑面に、その折詠んだ漢詩文が刻まれている。この試演で弾丸は目標地の一重山を飛び越え、不運にも幕府領で ある満照寺に着弾した。この一件で、幕府側と一悶着を引き起こした。

Fig. 40 Monument at the site of Shozan's cannon firing test
(Ikigaya, Chikuma City)
In the spring of 1851, Sakuma Shozan held a cannon firing test at Ikigaya, within the territory of the Matsushiro Domain. The text of a Chinese poem he composed at that time is written on this monument.
A cannonball fired during the test flew beyond the target of Mount Hitoe and landed at Manshō-ji Temple in shogunate territory. This incident led to a minor dispute with the government authorities.

図.41 徳川斉昭公(1800〜1860)
Fig. 41 Tokugawa Nariaki (1800-1860)

図. 42 徳川斉昭筆の『玉御絵』
徳川時代の親藩大名、水戸藩第九代藩主、徳川慶喜第十五代将軍の父。
諱号は「烈公」。強烈な攘夷論者で、大砲の弾を描いて、歌を詠んだものとみられる。
「ぬるがうちも 夢にみつ帆のえみし船、くだかむ 玉そ たから成ける」

Fig. 42 *Tama Gyoe* ("Cannonball Picture") by Tokugawa Nariaki
As 9th Head of the Mito Domain, Tokugawa Nariaki was one of the *shinpan daimyo* (feudal lords related to the Tokugawa shoguns). His son was the 15th shogun Tokugawa Keiki. His real name was "Rekko". A fierce campaigner in the *Joi* (expelling foreigners) faction, he is thought to have painted the cannonball first, then composed the poem.

*Nuruga uchi mo   yume ni mitsu ho no emishi fune
    kudakamu tama so takara narikeru*

("As I slept, I dreamed of a barbarian ship with three sails
A cannonball destroyed it and became a treasure* indeed")
*A play on the word *tama*, which can mean both "cannonball" and "jewel".

図.43 徳川斉昭の和歌・短冊「つつつつを」
西洋砲術に興味のあった烈公の和歌。
"大砲を連発するとき"と題されている。

「つつつつを、つらねつつうつ　つつつつは
　つつつつ毎に音はかりつつ　斉昭」

（最初の「つつつつ」は　筒筒、二句目最後の「うつ」は撃つ、
三句目、四句目の「つつつつ」は最初と同じ）

Fig. 43 Tanzaku poem "*Tsutsu tsutsu wo*" by Tokugawa Nariaki

A poem composed by Rekko, who was interested in western gunnery. The title mimics the sound made when cannons are fired in succession.
Tsutsu tsutsu wo   tsuranetsutsu utsu tsutsu tsutsu wa Tsutsu tsutsu goto ni oto kaharitsutsu— Nariaki
("Cannon, cannon, firing in succession, Cannon, cannon, changing their sound each time they are fired")

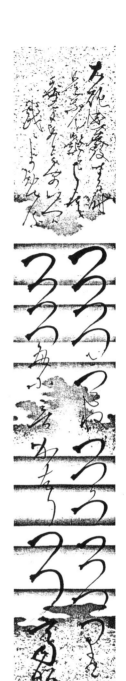

図. 44　佐久間象山宛書簡（象山神社）
一橋慶喜の屋敷へ象山を招聘するための書翰。
慶喜（徳川第15代将軍）は徳川斉昭の息子であった。このほか、象山は京都在住中に山階宮（幕末期の日本の皇族）などとも意見を交わしている。

Fig. 44 Letter to Sakuma Shozan (Zozan Shrine)

A letter inviting Shozan to the mansion of Nariaki's son Hitotsubashi Yoshinobu. Shozan also had discussions with Prince Yamashina and others while resident in Kyoto.

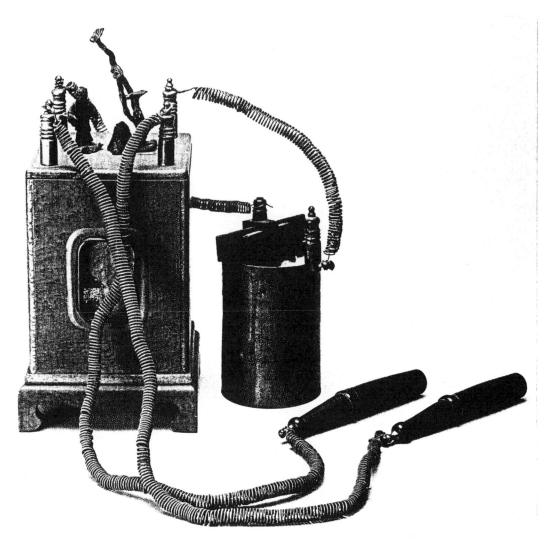

図. 45 電気治療器（真田宝物館蔵）
佐久間象山作と伝わるこの電気治療器は、彼が「エレキトロ・スコックマシネ」と表現した万延元年（1860）の頃のもの。他にも（逓信総合博物館蔵）、（長野市立松代小学校蔵）など何台かある。電気治療器は人間の不定愁訴などに効果があるとされる欧州の書物に関心をもった象山が「モノつくり」したもの。

Fig. 45 Electric therapy machine (Sanada Treasure Museum)
An electric therapy machine said to have been made by Sakuma Shozan, from around 1860 (when he described it as an *erekitoro sukokku mashine* or "electric shock machine"). There are several other versions, such as the ones kept at the Communications Museum and the Nagano City Matsushiro Elementary School. Electric therapy machines are examples of Shozan's manufacture of devices, revealing his interest in European books that explain their efficacy in treating health complaints of unknown cause.

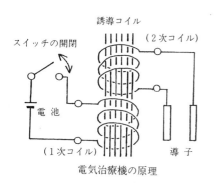

調査した誘導コイル　　　巻き線をほどいた誘導コイル

電気治療機の原理

調査した誘導コイルの電気的特性

	1次コイル	2次コイル
巻き数	514回	647回
自己インダクタンス	27.9mH	44.3mH
抵抗	3.7Ω	22.1Ω

図.46 誘導コイルと電気治療器の作用機序

電気を発生させるには一つは「エレキテル」と呼ばれる摩擦電気の利用、二つは日本で「ガルハニ」と呼ばれるボルタの電堆を使ったもの、三つ目は電磁誘導を利用する方法があることは知られていた（文献99）。象山の電気治療器は誘導コイルと電池を用いて電気的ショックを与えるもので一次側に電池を接続し、二次側に導子とよばれる金属パイプを接続させるタイプを製作。図は佐久間象山が製作したと伝えられる何台かの電気治療器の原理、及び澤田平所蔵の装置を分解調査した誘導コイル、巻線をほどいた誘導コイル、並びにその電気的特性を示したもの。数百kΩ以上あり、この誘導コイルでも十分「ビリビリ」と感じることができる旨、東徹（文献.16）が報告している。

Fig. 46 Induction coils and mechanism of an electric therapy machine

There were three known ways of generating electricity. The first was by using a triboelectric device (static electricity generator) called an "Elekiter", the second was by using a voltaic pile called "Garuhani" in Japan (after Luigi Galvani), and the third was by using electromagnetic induction (see Ref. 99). In Shozan's electric therapy machine, an induction coil and a battery were used to give an electric shock, with the primary side connected to the battery and the secondary side to a metal pipe called an electrode or director (*dōshi*). The diagram on the left shows the principle used in several electric therapy machines allegedly made by Sakuma Shozan. On the right, an induction coil dismantled and researched from a device in Taira Sawada's collection, an induction coil with the wire unwound, and the electrical properties of each. Toru Azuma (see Ref. 16) reports that these produced resistance measuring hundreds of kΩ or more, and that even with these coils there was a sufficient feeling of electric current passing through.

図. 47 絹巻銅線（逓信総合博物館）
象山が製作したとされる絹巻き銅線。箱の内部に「嘉永二年頃、象山が電機にしようしたもの」との記載がある。この銅線が電信実験に使われたもので、その年代が実験の年とされてきた。

Fig. 47 Silk-covered copper wire (Communications Museum)
Also thought to have been created by Shozan. Inside the box is an inscription stating "Used by Shozan for an electrical device in around 1849". The wire was used in a telegraph experiment, and the year inscribed on the box is assumed to be the year of the experiment.

図.48 測量用水準器
　箱書には「弘化三年丙午春、佐久間修理命大野源蔵造之」とあり、佐久間象山が大野源蔵に作らせたものであることがわかる。

Fig. 48 Water level for surveying
The inscription on the box reveals that Sakuma Shozan had this device made by Ono Genzo.

図.49 地震予知器
日本が頻繁に地震がおきる地震大国であることは当時も同じであった。このため小型の馬蹄形磁石を用い地震予知器と分類されたもの。地震が起きる前には磁力でくっついている鉄片が、地震で離れるという原理。象山が製作した磁石には、平板の磁石と、絹巻き導線を馬蹄形の鉄にコイル状とし、磁石としたものがある。

Fig. 49 Earthquake detector
Then, just as now, Japan was a country where massive earthquakes frequently occurred. This device is classified as an earthquake detector using a small horseshoe magnet. The basic principle was that an iron piece attached by magnetism would fall away due to earthquake motion. Some of Shozan's magnets were flat, while others were formed by coiling silk-covered copper wire around a horseshoe-shaped iron piece.

図.50 佐久間象山書簡　横田作大夫宛（逓信総合博物館）
　象山が門弟の横田作大夫に宛てた書翰。自分が製作した地震予知器については、その出来によって対価で分け与えると記す。地震予知器が金銭によって分けられていたことが分かる。

Fig. 50 Letter from Sakuma Shozan to Yokota Sakudayu
(Communications Museum)
A letter written by Shozan to his pupil Yokota Sakudayu. In it, he says that the earthquake detectors he has made will be priced according to their output. This reveals that earthquake detectors were classified in monetary terms.

Shozan and his wife Jun (1834〜1907)

図.51 コレラ意見書
　妻の順はコレラに罹り、電気治療器によって快方に向かっていた。象山はコレラに対しても興味を持っていた。コレラ撲滅のためには、火葬を禁止するべきなどの意見を述べている。

Fig. 51 Opinion on cholera
When Shozan's wife Jun contracted cholera, her condition was improved with the aid of an electric therapy machine. Shozan was also interested in cholera. Here, he states his opinion that cremations should be banned in order to eradicate the disease.

第121代天皇

孝明天皇

在位期間
1846年3月10日-1867年1月30日

Emperor Komei (1831～1867)

the period of Emperor reign
Mar.10.1846＿Jan.30.1867

図. 52『桜賦』象山 50 歳の書
中国・春秋戦国時代の楚の政治家・屈原(BC343〜BC278)が作品化した「橘」の詩に発想を得て、象山は「桜」を詠んだ。開国の志を抱いたが、その意は幕府に通じず、悶々として蟄居の身に暮れていた。憂国至誠の情に煩悶しながら、象山は自らを深山の桜を擬して心情を語っている。賦の大意は「桜花が日本の名花である如く、私も国に対し比類のない卓見を懐いている。開国して外国の技芸を取り入れることが唯一の国防の策であるが、攘夷論が天下を動かしているのは憂慮に堪えない。今ここにおいて頼るのは皇室である。私の意を採用して開国の国是を確立して戴きたい」。「桜花」は百花に優る徳をたたえているとした、象山の自負が横溢としている。文久 2 年(1862)に孝明天皇の展覧に供されている。

Fig. 52 *Sakura no Fu* ("Prose Poem on Cherry Blossom") written when Shozan was 50

Shozan's inspiration for this prose poem came from 橘頌 *Ju Song* ("In Praise of the Orange-Tree"), a poem by the Chu politician Qu Yuan (343-278 BC) during China's Warring States period. Shozan's fervent wish was that Japan's national seclusion should end, but his sentiments were not shared by the shogunate, causing him to live with the frustration of house arrest. While agonizing over his feelings of patriotism, Shozan describes his mental state by comparing it to a wild cherry tree deep in the mountains. The poem can be broadly interpreted as follows. "Just as the cherry blossom is a characteristic flower of Japan, I too have an ambition of unparalleled excellence for my country. My proposal is that our only form of national defence is to open up the country and introduce foreign technology. But the campaign to expel foreigners is building momentum, and this causes me unbearable anxiety. One thing we can depend upon is our Imperial line. I hope my sentiments will be shared and a national policy of ending seclusion will be established". In praising cherry blossom as having virtue in excess of all other flowers, Shozan is bursting with pride. The poem was presented for viewing by the Emperor Komei in 1862.

図.53 水墨山水図
　　（松代の代々の豪商・第11代八田慎蔵氏蔵）
安政四年（1857年）象山が松代に蟄居していた時代、松代の豪商・八田子静（第6代八田慎蔵）のすすめに応じて描いた山水画。象山の数少ない水墨画である。

Fig. 53 Landscape painting in water-ink (Collection of Hatta Shinzo, 11th generation in a line of wealthy merchants from Matsushiro)
A landscape painted at the request of Hatta Shisei, 6th generation of Hatta Shinzo wealthy merchants from Matsushiro, while Shozan was under house arrest in Matsushiro in 1857. Of all Shozan's works, this is a rare water-ink painting.

図.54 象山淨稿（京都大学付属図書館）
象山が松代において蟄居中に、自身が書きとめた詩の類を纏めたもの。象山の思想面を考究する上で重要な資料となっている。

Fig. 54 *Shozan Jōkō* ("Texts by Shozan", Kyoto University Library)
A collection of poetic works written by Shozan while under house arrest in Matsushiro. This is an important resource for analyzing Shozan's thought.

図.55 佐久間象山宛書状（象山神社）
象山が松代での蟄居を免ぜられると、幕府から上洛するようにとの命令を受ける。この後、京都での活躍が始まる。

Fig. 55 Letter to Sakuma Shozan (Zozan Shrine)
In this letter, Shozan is released from house arrest in Matsushiro and ordered by the shogunate to proceed to the capital. His activity in Kyoto starts from this time.

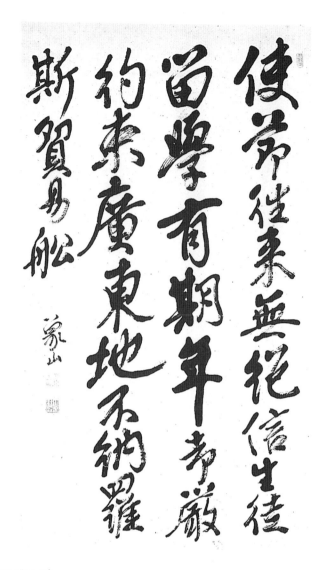

図.56 雑感七絶
箱書によれば、象山が元治元年(1864年)門人の河原理助に与えたもの。
象山最晩年の作品。

Fig. 56 *Zakkan Shichizetsu* ("Miscellaneous Thoughts in a Seven-Syllable Quatrain")
The inscription on the box reveals that Shozan gave this poem to his follower Kawahara Risuke in 1864. One of Shozan's final works.

図. 57 佐久間象山書簡　勝海舟宛（象山神社）
象山が凶刃に倒れる少し前に書かれた書翰。勝海舟は、この書翰に続けて象山から受け取った最後の書翰であることを記している。

Fig. 57 Letter from Sakuma Shozan to Katsu Kaishu (Zozan Shrine)
A letter written shortly before Shozan was assassinated. At the bottom, Katsu Kaishu adds a note to say that this was the last letter he received from Shozan.

図. 58 馬具（ゼッケ）
象山は早くから西洋馬具を好んで使っており危険性を指摘されてきた。これは象山が凶刃に倒れた際に馬に付けられていた西洋式の馬具（ゼッケ）である。象山の血がついている。

Fig. 58 Saddlecloth
Shozan had long been a fan of western horse gear, though the dangers had been pointed out. This is the western-style saddlecloth used by Shozan when he was assassinated. It has traces of Shozan's blood on it.

図. 59 斬奸状

象山が京都で暗殺された日、三条大橋に掲げられたもの。翌日、三沢刑部丞らが密かに剥ぎ取って持って帰って来たという。象山を殺害したことを正当化している。

Fig. 59 *Zankanjō* ("Criminal Indictment")

This was posted on Sanjo Ohashi bridge on the day Shozan was assassinated in Kyoto. A group of men including a police official named Misawa are said to have secretly torn it down and taken it away the following day. It justifies the murder of Shozan.

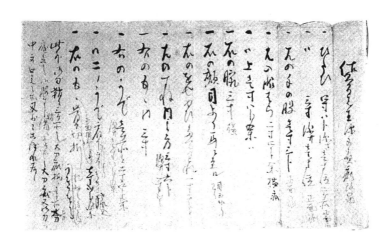

図. 60 佐久間象山深手疵改

象山が凶刃に倒れた際の傷跡についての調書。

Fig. 60 *Sakuma Shozan Fukade Kizuaratame* ("Investigation of the Grievous Injuries of Sakuma Shozan")

A report describing the injuries sustained by Shozan when he was assassinated.

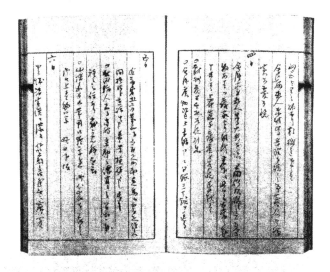

図.61 海舟日記 （東京都江戸東京博物館）
慶応二年（1866）7月5日、行方の分からなくなっていた象山の息子である恪二郎は、新撰組の近藤勇らのもとに居たことが分かり、そのお礼をしたと勝海舟は記している。

Fig. 61 Kaishu's Diary (Edo-Tokyo Museum)
Shozan's son Kakujiro went missing on July 5, 1866, but was eventually found safe in the protection of Kondo Isami, commander of the Shinsengumi vigilantes. Katsu Kaishu writes on discovering this, and expresses his gratitude.

図.62 土方歳蔵書簡 勝海舟宛 （東京都江戸東京博物館）
象山の息子・恪二郎（三浦敬之助）は、父・象山の仇を討つため新撰組に入隊したという。新撰組の土方歳三は、文武研究に励むように説得したと、伯父の勝海舟に手紙で知らせた。

Fig. 62 Letter from Hijikata Toshizo to Katsu Kaishu (Edo-Tokyo Museum)
A letter informing Kaishu that Shozan's son Kakujiro (Miura Keinosuke) has joined the Shinsengumi vigilantes to avenge his father's death. Hijikata Toshizo, a leading member of the Shinsengumi, explains that he has persuaded Kakujiro to immerse himself in studying literature and martial arts.

図.63 京都維新史跡のうち佐久間象山遭難地
　　（京都大学附属図書館）

象山が遭難（暗殺）された場所である京都木屋町付近の写真。近代になってからの写真。

Fig. 63 The site of Sakuma Shozan's assassination, one of Kyoto's Meiji Restoration Sites (Kyoto University Library)
A photograph of the Kiyamachi neighbourhood, where Shozan was assassinated. The photograph dates from the Modern era.

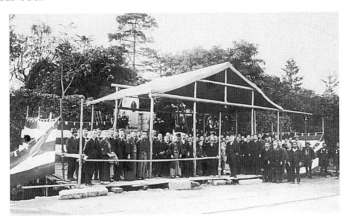

図.64 象山遭難碑除幕祈念写真(個人)

大正四年（1915年）十月三十一日、「佐久間象山先生記念塔」完成記念の除幕式が行われた。記念写真中央には、象山遭難時の目撃者である田中とくさんが写っている。

Fig. 64 Commemorative Photograph on the Unveiling of the Shozan Assassination Monument (privately owned)
On October 31st, 1915, an unveiling ceremony was held to mark the completion of the "Sakuma Shozan Memorial Tower". Toku Tanaka, who witnessed the assassination, can be seen in the centre of the photograph.

図.65『省諐録』碑
（松代町象山神社）

余年（よとし）二十以後は乃（すなわ）ち匹夫（ひっぷ）も一国に繋（かか）ることあるを知る。三十以後は乃ち天下の繋ることあるを知る。
四十以後は乃ち五世界に繋ることあるを知る。

Fig. 65 *Seikenroku* Monument
(Zozan Shrine, Matsushiro-cho)

When I was 20,
 I could act and think on the scale of a whole domain.
At 30, I knew how to act and think on the scale of Japan.
Today, at past 40,
I must think on a global scale, and act with appropriate magnanimity.

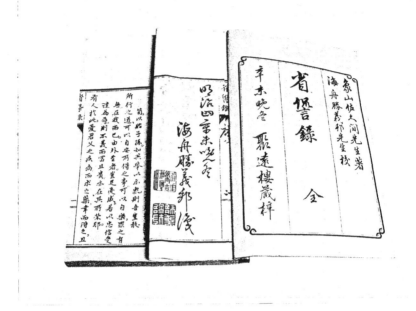

図. 66 『省諐録』(真田幸俊氏寄託)
松代にて蟄居中に、象山が書き記した書。本書の出版は象山暗殺後、明治になってから勝海舟の出資などを基に発刊の運びとなった。

Fig. 66 *Seikenroku* ("Record of Conscience") (by kind permission of Mr Yukitoshi Sanada)
A work written by Shozan while under house arrest in Matsushiro. It was not published until the Meiji period, after Shozan's assassination, with funding provided by Katsu Kaishu.

＊勝海舟と『省諐録』上梓

　勝海舟(1823〜1899){通称:麟太郎、諱は義邦、号は海舟、明治維新後は安房}は江戸の旗本の子として生まれ。江戸時代末期から明治維新にかけての幕臣、政治家。1860年に咸臨丸で渡米し、帰国後軍艦奉行、幕府軍の軍事総裁となり、山岡鉄舟(1836〜1888)、髙橋泥舟 (1835〜1903) と共に江戸無血開城を成功裡に実現させた。勝海舟は明治維新後には枢密顧問官、伯爵になり、山岡鉄舟は明治天皇の侍従になり、髙橋泥舟は将軍徳川慶喜の護衛役に徹した。象山の弟子・海舟は蘭学修行時代に蘭語辞書「ズーフ・ハルマ」を1年かけて2部筆写した有名な逸話があり、一部は自分用、一部は売ってカネを得る商才を示した。海舟は象山の知遇を得、後に妹・お順は象山の正妻となった。　象山が暗殺された直後の海舟の衝撃、痛憤は極大となり、象山を『蓋世の英雄』と呼んだ。象山暗殺後は遺児・恪二郎の後見人となり、会津藩（京都守護職）の公用役であった山本覚馬に任せ、養育費を出し、新撰組預りとさせた。海舟は象山の死後、『省諐録』などをはじめ遺稿を妹のお順や、恪二郎から預かった。その後、明治3年、佐久間家の家名再興の許可が下りたのを契機として、この『省諐録』は海舟が幕臣・軍艦奉行だった木村芥舟(1830〜1901)へ依頼し、上梓の運びとなった。因みに勝海舟、山岡鉄舟、髙橋泥舟を『幕末の三舟』と呼ばれることがあるが、この木村芥舟を入れて『幕末の四舟』と言われることもある。

*On Katsu Kaishu and "Record of Conscience"

Katsu Kaishu (1823-1899) was born the son of a Tokugawa retainer in Edo. His childhood name was Rintaro, his real name was Yoshikuni, his pseudonym was Kaishu, and he changed his name to Yasuyoshi after the Meiji Restoration. He was a politician and government minister from the end of the Edo period to the Meiji Restoration.

In 1860, he travelled to the United States in the *Kanrin Maru*. After his return to Japan, he served as a warship commander and naval commissioner of the shogunate forces, and together with Yamaoka Tesshu (1836-1888) and Takahashi Deishu (1835-1903) successfully ensured the peaceful surrender of Edo Castle. After the Meiji Restoration, he served on the Privy Council and was elevated to the title of *Hakushaku* (Count), while Yamaoka Tesshu became the Emperor Meiji's chamberlain and Takahashi Deishu served as a personal guard to the shogun Tokugawa Yoshinobu.

A famous anecdote has Katsu Kaishu taking a year to write two copies of the "Doeff-Halma" Dutch dictionary as a student of Dutch learning. He kept one copy for himself and sold the other, showing a certain acumen for earning money. It was during this time that he entered favour with Sakuma Shozan, who would later marry his younger sister O-Jun.

In his shock and immense indignation immediately after Shozan's assassination, he called Shozan "the mightiest hero". After the assassination, he became the guardian of Shozan's son Kakutaro, and entrusted him to the safekeeping of Yamamoto Kakuma, a public official in the Aizu Domain (Military Commissioner of Kyoto). He paid the expenses for the boy's upkeep and placed him in the custody of the Shinsengumi vigilantes.

After Shozan's death, Kaishu obtained Shozan's remaining manuscripts including *Seikenroku* from O-Jun and Kakutaro. Then, in 1870, when permission was granted for the Sakuma family name to be revived, he had *Seikenroku* published by Kimura Kaishu (1830-1901), the former shogunate minister and warship commander. Incidentally, Katsu Kaishu, Yamaoka Tesshu and Takahashi Deishu are generally known as the "Bakumatsu Three *Shu*" on account of their names, but with the addition of Kimura Kaishu, they are sometimes called the "Bakumatsu Four *Shu*".
(Shu means boat)

◇省警録とは、あやまちをかえりみる記録という意味である。象山は吉田松陰の密航失敗事件に連坐して、江戸伝馬町の獄につながれていた。安政元年(一八五四)四月より九月まで、本書はその獄中での感懐を出獄後に筆録したものである。内容は多岐にわたるが、それまでの自己の思想と行動をふりかえりながら、その道徳的および思想的正当性を主張することが、眼目となっている。

警起 わが身をいましめふるいたつ。

余が親姻 勝海舟の妹順子が象山の妻であった。

厄に遭へり 象山は元治元年(一八六四)七月一一日に尊攘派によって暗殺された。海舟は、これと松陰密航事件への連坐とを混同しているようにみえる。

筐底 はこのそこ。

悋 悋二郎。妾菊の出で嘉永元年(一八四八)生れ。象山には妾腹の子が三男一女あったが、彼以外は夭折している。

連累 象山の暗殺後、佐久間家は知行および家屋敷を没収され、悋二郎は浪人となった。なお、悋二郎は明治三年(一八七〇)に赦され、家禄七〇石を給され、同六年に司法省に出仕するが、明治一〇年に死去した。

流離顚沛 さまよい、くるしい境遇にあること。

上木 出版。

　　　　序

　花の春に先だつものは、残霜の傷ふところとなり、説の時に先だつものは、旧弊の厄しむるところとなる。しかりといへども、先だつものあらずんば、すなはち後るるものの何をもって*警起せんや。余が*親姻、象山佐久間翁は開化日新の説を先唱し、数年前において終に*厄に遭へり。厄に遭ふの中、数章を筆し省警録と題し*筐底に蔵す。このごろ携へ来りて余に示す。*流離顚沛の間にこの遺稿を守れり。厄に遭ふを免れず。今の世の人、もしこの書をもって木す。ああ、説の衆に魁くるものは厄に遭ふものとなさんか、すなはち余はまさに日はんとす、子の見識のここに至れるは、あに厄に遭へるものの賜にあらずやと。因りて資を助けて*上木す。平々にして奇なしとなさんか、すなはち余はまさに日はんとす、子の見識のここに至れるは、あに厄に遭へるものの*賜にあらずやと。

　　　明治四辛未晩冬

　　　　　　　　海舟勝義邦識す

省諐録・原文

Original Text by Chinese Classical Literature

省諐錄

象山平大星啓　又名子明氏

嘉永甲寅。夏四月。大星以事下獄。在繋七月。省愆之餘。弗無所述。然獄中禁筆研。不能存藁。故久而多忘。既出而錄其所臆記。藏諸巾笥以貽子孫。如其舉以示衆則吾豈敢。

所行之道。可以自安。所得之事。可以自樂。罪之有無。在我而已。由外至者。豈足憂戚。若以忠信受譴爲辱。則不義而富且貴。亦在其所榮耶。

有人於此。憂君父之疾病。而求之藥。幸而得之。且知其必有效也。則不問其品之貴賤。名之美惡。必請之於君父矣。君父惡其名而不許。則多方謀之。竊有之乎。抑亦坐而俟其啓手足歟。臣子至誠惻怛之情。固不可坐視其病患。則雖知後逢其怒。亦豈得不竊進之哉。

人所不及知而我獨知之。人所不及能而我獨能之。是亦荷天之寵也。荷天之寵如此。而惟爲一身計。不爲天下計。則其負天也豈不亦大乎。

自古懷忠被罪者。何限。吾無怨焉。但猶可及爲之時。而不爲將使病弊至於不可復救。是則可悲已。

縱予今日死。天下後世當有公論。予又何悔何恨。

身雖在囹圄。心無愧怍。自覺方寸虛明。不異平日。人心之靈。與天地上下同流。夷狄患難累他不得。亦可驗也。惟北闕年滿八十。飲食坐臥。非予不安。自予逮繫。音問不通。動靜不知。其憂慮苦悶。當如何哉。一念及之。尤難爲情。然亦以理排遣。不至累心。

吾不履此境。無此省覺。經一跌。長一知。果非虛語。

振拔特立可也。激昂忿戾。不可也。

心戒走作。

心曰秉。日操。亦是時時提撕以理勝之之謂。

吾雖久從事格物內而家庭外而鄉黨親朋。異時停調處置。頗以爲當者。徐而省之往往有大過不及不滿人意。皆是工夫未熟人情世故未得通徹故也。可不策勵哉。

格物之於天地造化卻易。於人情世故卻難。吾人須不可狃其所易而倦其所難。

行身規矩則不可不嚴。此治己之方也。治人。待人規矩則不可過嚴。此安人之道也。安人卽所以自安。

凡讀書須熟誦不然。無甚受用。予來此中書卷不得攜與端居書室左右廚子。所欲檢查輒隨手抽繹。全然不同。日日默念。而因以爲藥石爲針砭者不過平素所精讀暗記者。少時專務博涉多讀羣書。率皆若存若亡。今欲記起而卒不能雖多亦奚以爲。他日幸得放還。當以諗後生且以自警也。

予自來此、勉勵克治、鍛鍊身心、未嘗虛度時日。古人云、儻閒居眞不空過日月。彼錮我者皆成我也、旨哉。

予雖門葉衰薄、亦生長飽暖之中、未經牢鍊寒苦之境、常恐一旦國家緩急起居飲食、多所不勝。然去夏彌利堅艦突至江都戒嚴、予爲藩邸經理軍務、不得睡者七晝夜、精神倍奮。今歲得罪下獄、飯糲食、嚼鹽、與重囚爲伍、數旬恬然安之、精神活潑、身亦健康、此二事少自試驗、得盆不細、亦可謂天之賜矣。

外邪襲人、多在睡眠之時、故中夜就寢、不得熟眠、爲令速寢、常當係意在醒若支體有所不安、或隨意轉側、務令血氣無所停滯、若咽喉不滑、或運舌嚥津、或深息閉氣、少焉放之、如是行之、外邪亦侵不得。

內定心志、外運血氣、晝節飲食、夜少睡眠、修養妙訣、果無多子。

聞關西地震、勢賀之閒更甚、城垣衙署驛亭民屋傾塌無算、樹木倒植井水乾涸、人民壓死、殆不知其數、丁未信州地大震、予在鄉里、親閱其變、慘毒之劇、

張泓所著滇南新語關西地震在六月十四日。而獄中傳之。在二十四五日間。季秋放還後。次第此錄。至十一月四日。東海道地又大震。燦城郭。壞廬舎。死傷無數。因竊書寄於江都所親。告以此依大意。謂都下恐亦不免。

所不忍言。信中變後。地下每作雷聲。時亦搖撼。經久不止。後七年有小田原之變。又一年。今復有關西之變。嘗記淸人雜書所載云其地常動。至數年後有大震。萬家樂土。忽變蠻叢。然則地震固有連數年者矣。古來漢儒以地震爲蠻夷侵陵之兆占候之說洋學所不取。雖然天人合應之理。不可謂必無之。丁未以來。地震之變以時事驗之漢儒之言似不可誣。今夷虜之志。未知其所極。則震之相連。而尚有劇甚者。亦不能無慮焉。

君子有五樂。而富貴不與焉。一門知禮義。骨肉無釁隙二樂也。取予不苟。廉潔自養。內不愧於妻孥。外不怍於衆民二樂也。講明聖學。心識大道。隨時安義。處險如夷。三樂也。生乎西人啓理窟之後。而知古聖賢所未嘗識之理。四樂也。東洋道德。西洋藝術精粗不遺。表裏兼該。因以澤民物。報國恩五樂也。

抗孔聖浮雲之志。養鄒叟浩然之氣。寵辱不驚。俛仰不怍。究天地之際。觀古今之變。玩萬物之理。稽人身之紀。雖在困極。樂亦有在焉。饑而食。渴而飮。坐而

思倦而睡。迨然自得。又不知身在圜牆之中矣。

倦之平素有所戒備。明年十月二日夜。江都果有大震。火又從之。其餘烈比之前之數災超過數倍矣。而予舊所親交多得保全。雖是天意亦不無小資於予焉。乙卯冬記。

敏一字。是爲學之法。而爲治之要。亦莫若焉。天下可學可爲之務。如此其廣。如彼其大。故學與治。皆不可以不敏。彼終身于學。而空疎無用終身于官。而因仍無功者。坐其勤力不敏。十常八九。

孔子之聖猶且發憤忘食。敏以求之。何況吾輩。

日晷一移千載無再來之今。形神既離萬古無再生之我。學藝事業。豈可悠悠射有禮射武射之別。然其初一也。故其生。桑弧蓬矢以射天地四方。然後敢用穀。亦第一義也。專爲防禦而設防禦之事。蓋男子立身第一義也。故男子生乎今之世。不知銃礮。其可乎於其初生亦宜以礮換弧矢發於上下四方。以志於其所有事也。

弓矢長兵。皆失其爲利男子生乎今之世。不知銃礮。亦非常之原。常人異焉耳。

予久畱意於海防。其所發明。自謂前人有未及者。然卒由此取禍。

君相如有省悟時則吾志之行必矣。

凡學問必以積累、非一朝一夕之所能通曉。海防利害、亦是一大學問、自非講究有素者、未易遽得其要領。人雖提耳告之、而不解。蓋亦由此。不令外夷開易侮之心、是防禦之至要也。邊海防堵、皆不得其法。所陳銃器、皆不中其式。所接官吏、皆凡夫庸人。胸無甲兵、如此而欲無開夷人侮心、寧可得乎。

有敵國外患、而託本根未固、形勢未成、進無果決之勇、退持遷延之計者、其所欲糜敵、適足以啓敵而自糜。其所欲緩寇、適足以資寇而自緩。其所欲從容補綴、而全其捍禦之備者、亦將徒爲文具、而國家之勢、愈至於不可支矣。而古來當局者、曾不深省、誤家國天下、如出一塗、可勝歎哉。

今之當將帥之任者、非公侯貴人、卽膏梁氏族。平日以飲酒歌舞爲娛、不知兵謀師律爲何事、一旦有國家之急、誰能爲軍士之所服、而遏敵人之衝突、是

今之深患也。故予嘗欲倣西洋武備之大略、於天下兵籍外結故家世族忠勇剛毅、一可當十者、以爲義會、以保國護民爲志。其初入會、校試稽效、不憚艱苦、方始聽入焉。推有韜略謀猷統馭之才者爲之長、遇警急之日、則鳩集成師、以待官之指揮。庶乎攘寇植勳、或居於在兵籍者之上也。

欲戰必勝、不守必固、不可。欲守必固、不陣必定、不可。魏侯問陣必定之道、吳子曰、君能使賢者居上、不肖者處下、則陣已定矣。今天下諸國、賢者未必居上、不肖者未必處下。然則陣未定也。陣未定而其守必固、戰必勝者、未之有也。

有志之主、尚其知所警省哉。

教練不精、賞罰不明、又無能用之者、縱有億萬之衆、其於戰守、所謂伏鷄乳犬。如其貍與虎何哉。

同力度德、同德量義、雖稱文王之美、亦不過云大國畏其力、小國懷其德。無其力而能保其國者、自古至今、吾未之見也。誰謂王者不尚力耶。

不知彼。不知己。每戰必敗固也。然知彼知己。在今時未可言戰。悉善彼之所善。而不喪己之所能然後始可以言戰。詳證術。萬學之基本也。泰西發明此術兵略亦大進。貸然與往時別。所謂下學而上達也。孫子兵法度量數稱勝。亦其術也。然漢與我有孫子以來莫不誦習而講說。而其兵法依然如舊不得與泰西比肩。是無他。坐於無下學之功也。今眞欲修飭武備非先興此學科不可。

士大夫必有過人之膽量方能奪戎狄之氣而伸本國之威。如郭汾陽之單騎見虜。是矣。必有過人之學問才辯。而能屈戎狄之辭。而存本國之體。如富文忠之卻獻納二字是矣。今天朝縉紳數與夷使接者果有汾陽之膽量乎。果有文忠之學問才辯乎。吾竊危之。

人不見其可畏。則必慢易之。一啓其慢易之心。又何以能治之也。故君子必臨之以莊。正其衣冠。尊其瞻視。出辭氣斯遠鄙倍皆所以爲莊之方也。今士大

夫往往有舉措輕佻。言辭鄙猥以自喜者。其意蓋謂不如是難以通人情而服人。嗟乎通人情而服人者。自有其道在焉。今不以其道而露此醜態吾恐其欲服人者。適足以導其慢易也。

人譽已於已何加。若因譽而自怠則反損。人毀已於已何損。若因毀而自強則反益。

有人之過。有事之過。未可以觀人。人之過可以觀人。

今之所謂儒者。果何爲者耶。本朝神聖造國之道。堯舜三代帝王之治。彙明而默識之乎。禮樂刑政。典章制度。以至兵法師律械器之利。講論而皆得其要乎。土境之形勢。海陸道路之險夷。外蕃之情狀。防戍之利害。城堡堵堞控援之略。推算重力幾何。詳證之術。並究而悉之乎。吾未之知也。然則今之所謂儒者。果何爲者耶。

讀書講學。徒爲空言不及當世之務。與淸談廢事。一閒耳。

107

有之、無所補、無之無所損、乃無用之學也、有用之學、譬如夏時之葛、冬時之裘、
脫無爲之者、則生民之用闕矣、
帝王之政、藏財於民、有餘而取、不足而與、故不凍餒、百姓而上獨富、足亦不飽
逸百姓、而國獨貧寠、故曰百姓足、君孰與不足、百姓不足、君孰與足、此天下
古今不易之道也、
本邦金貨米粟、號爲富饒、然疆域不大、故以邦內所生之財、享邦內所爲之用、
無不有餘、乃若海防之事、則起于外者也、置防堵數百所、造大艦數百艘、鑄
瓦礟數千門、其費亦浩矣、而皆非永存之物、每一二十年、必待修繕改造、況
外之有應接給資之用、內之有餉糧購買之費、凡如此之類、將安取其給哉、
夫劣濟困窮之家、多得賓客、屢設宴饗、則其資財空乏、卒至於不可復繼也
必矣、今之時事、何以異乎、是然則其所以經理之者、何術有志於經世者、所
（宜先審計一）

木版本購買に作る。今購買に改む。

予礦卦之著不但有益於武學生徒兼有裨於國家武備往日官阻其鑴版吾不知其何意。

先公登相臺嗣管防海事時英夷寇清國聲勢相逮予感慨時事之所著而其書之序。天保壬寅十一月也後觀清魏源聖武記亦感慨時事之所著而其書之序。又作於是歲之七月則先予上書蓋四月矣。而其所論往往有不約而同者。嗚乎。予與魏各生異域不相識姓名感時著言同在是歲。而其所見亦有闇合者。一何奇也眞可謂海外同志矣。但魏云。自上世以來中國有海防。而無海戰。遂以堅壁淸野。杜絕岸奸爲防海家法。予則欲盛講礮艦之術。而爲邀擊之計。驅逐防截。以制賊死命於外海。是爲異耳。

馭夷俗者。莫如先知夷情。知夷情者。莫如先通夷語。故通夷語者。不惟爲知彼之楷梯。亦是馭彼之先務也。予竊深念頃年諸蕃託事屢寄舶於相房。開其情固爲難測。因有纂輯皇國同文鑑若干卷。以通歐羅諸國語之志。而荷蘭

久為五市之國。邦人亦多知讀其國書。故欲先刊荷蘭部。先是官有命。凡刊行書籍。必經官看詳。迺嘉永己酉冬。來江都。呈稿本以請。遷延彌年。卒不得允。其在江都日。始獲魏氏之書而讀之。亦欲內地設學專譯夷書夷史。瞭悉敵情以補於駕馭。是又其見之與予相符者。第不識彼國今日能用其言否耳。

海防之要。在礮與艦。而礮最居首。魏氏海國圖誌中。輯銃礮之說。類皆粗漏無稽。如兒童戲嬉之為。凡事不自為之。而能得其要領者無之。以魏之才識。而是之不察。當今之世。身無礮學。貽此謬妄。反誤後生。吾為魏深惜之。

去夏墨虜以兵艦四隻。護送其國書抵浦賀澳。其舉動詞氣殊極悖慢。辱國體不細。聞者莫不切齒。時某人鎮浦賀。屏氣負屈。遂無能為虜退後。自抽小刀。寸斷其所遺虜主畫像。以洩怒。昔宋曹瑋謫官陝西。聞趙元昊為人。乃使善畫者圖其貌。觀之知其英物。必為邊患。欲預講邊備。蒐閱人才。後果如其言。

然則觀其肖影。亦可以見其能否。而資吾豫備矣。某人知慮不及此。毀而滅之。可惜已。嗚乎。均夷人也。均畫像也。或無而求之。或有而毀之。其知之深淺。謀之長短。一何遠哉。

今春墨虜之來。官設便坐於橫濱。以爲應接之所。命松城小倉二藩發兵以護衞之。且令聽約束於接待官吏。初吾公之受命也。以爲眞備虜之不虞也。乃發野戰礮二門。牛角天礮三門。銃卒百名。刀槍士五十名。以國老望月貫恕督之。予參其軍議。謂接待官吏知兵令吾與小倉一橫一直以陣。銃手可以逞威。若其不知兵。使相對而陣。則銃不可用。惟短兵利之。與虜相接咫尺變起倉卒。彼雖精銃。技我以利兵乘之。一薙可斫斷數頭。乃別備長卷二十把。以從吾兵至金川。官吏使人謂曰。大礮必實前驛。莫引入橫濱地。望月對曰。吾藩奉命護衞應接之場。大礮所以備變。實之隔地。變發非時。難以應卒。敢辭。官吏曰。今兹應接。萬萬可保其無變。不幸將有變。卽時發官丁搬運礮器。

決不レ令下貴藩有二缺乏一今以二大礒一入二横濱一夷人或憚中其守衞之嚴上請レ移中於他地一官之累也。望月不レ得レ已從レ之。退日官命使二聽中約束一者幾是乎。及相二護衞之地一官吏曰。東起于二海涘一西行二百步。折而北行又如レ之。是其所也。予聞レ之驚駭。詳其地。南距二應接便坐一不レ下二二百步一有民屋樹林在二其閒一。初在二江戸一竊意官吏雖レ不レ語レ兵。自有二國體一。且得二二藩兵當密圍繞便坐一以嚴警禦不レ圖其區處之陋至レ斯也。因建議曰。大礒則官吏停レ之。今所二有者一小銃而已。小銃逞レ力。非二百步內一不レ可。且銃卒不レ踰二百名一執二短兵一者。不二過五十名一夷虜集會之所遠陣於二二百步之外一又散守二三四百步之閒一不レ惟無レ益於二警禦一適足二以導虜之侮慢一。去歲浦賀應接護衞無レ法。夷虜嗤レ之。而不二少省悟一今又爲二此兒戲一官吏不レ肯。固不レ足レ道。本藩武功盛名爲二此輩一壞隳。豈可レ忍邪。乃與望月謀。使二人謂一レ之曰。如公等所二區處一。是非下以二我兵備一於二夷虜一爲中夷虜禁二呵邦民一者上。固不レ可レ煩二士大夫一。亦無下用二於兵器一每二巡路一出中健兒一二名執上

青竹杖誰何之足矣。但江戶所受之命則不可以廢。應接之日。吾藩當別出士卒。整陣於山間。以備非時之變耳。此不敗公等之事。又不墜吾職。豈不亦兩得乎。官吏復曰。言皆當理。然官發兩藩人士之事。吾輩既告之。夷人亦若不出其人。設陣於隱僻之地。夷人必疑吾有異志。應接不諧。是亦官之累也。必曲從吾言。如其布陣收散離合。唯意所命。吾輩不敢掣肘。予與望月雖憤惋不樂。亦無可奈何。當日作一哨。置之田畝。閒以塞其責。嗚呼。耗損國用。勤勞士卒。盡思慮計畫而同為兒戲。可付浩歎也已。

二月廿日夜聞下田議略定。翌朝早起。詣望月曰。下田本邦要地。其形勢可比全世界之喜望峯。夷虜儼之屯駐以為巢穴。其害不可言。且大城在江戶。而人口眾多。米穀布帛皆資海運。不幸有警。海路格塞。江戶首受其禍。伊豆之為州。天城之險。隔絕其中。而下田在其南端。一旦變起。陸路出兵。礒隊為嶮所沮。不可以行。海路則我無堅艦。他日縱得造作。虜有海陸之形勝。而我反

喪之。主客易位。攻守殊勢。非計也。夫善制事者。常令其利在我。其害在彼。今不得已。而假敵人地。宜爲他日計。擇海陸得進兵之處。竊覽橫濱之地勢。甚稱之。且使虜舶常在此。去江戸甚邇。則人人嘗膽坐薪之念。自不能已。警衛守禦之方。亦自不得不嚴。又親觀彼之所長。可以速進我之智巧。是其所以爲多利。如退下田。則其爲江戸腹心之患則不能以髮故吾謂不如以橫濱假之之爲愈也。是天下之大計也。君總士卒在茲。不可以默。吾上書乞公有獻策可也。望月日然然吾上書不如子之上言。乃命予還江戸。告之於公有沮者不果。公許予自爲之。於是竊有所建白。又使門人長岡小林虎上書其主侯開陳大計又使之見阿部閣老所親幸爲論其利害欲得因時規諫有所挽回竝皆不行。小林生以此獲主侯之譴。遂辭歸國。
曩予偕二三友生。爲鎌倉之遊。遂泛海。過荒岬。抵城島。泊三崎。歷松輪。宿宮田。

次浦賀、上猿嶼、觀於金澤、出本牧而還、其往來所由、親設防堵備海寇、無慮十餘所、而錯置皆不得法、無一可當防截之選者、至此不覺仰天浩歎擗胸流涕者久之、夫江都天下之咽喉也、富津洲觜雖稱曰天險、海口猶闊、非有戰艦水軍、固難以過敵人侵擾窺伺、今是之不務、設爲癡堵呆堞、高揭之於海表、此示我無謀於海外也、頃年東西諸藩、寄舶遊偵、豈不開輕我之心哉、吏員庸流、固不足譴、其金鞍華韉、綾衣肉食、自謂高出等類者、不知天下之大計蘗國財用、以爲此無益之務、抑何歟、有如虜舶馳突、將何以折衝禦侮、因欲上疏論海防利病、冀以裨時政之萬一、具草請之先公、先公不許、遂止、是嘉永庚戌之首夏也、後四年果墨夷之事起、登時先公尼予上書者、蓋懼觸忤抵罪也、其蓋覆之仁、亦大矣、今日使先公在世、知予拘囚則其爲憂勞又當何如、

川路司農、自大阪市尹轉任、與聞防海事、予舊有厚交、因出擬上書舊稿示之、

極言近都防堵修築無法不適實用司農亦未甚信之及墨夷事興無一不如予嘗所論於是始深納予言一日謂予曰子欲有所言吾能達之於閣老予曰僕所欲言者爲君傾倒幾盡君能言之君能行之天下之福也僕但求天下之福耳上書釣名非其本心也及論選人材購船於海外之策司農有沮色予曰是當今先務之急而君猶牽掣故常不能發言他尙何望僕當上書以道之乃條疏急務十事因司農上之阿部閣老不報至吉田生獄起亦不少蒙明察故常之不易變時勢之不可明如此不知天下之大計將何日而能立也。

江戶海口不可無礮臺予亦嘗數數言之夫海口之防戰利在礮臺其形勢所缺不可不實此以補焉然其得力之處全在別備礮艦相機策應故能得其要海中唯置一二區而足不必多築之荷蘭諳厄兒之策可據也如今所爲陸續相連是陸軍爲壘以自屛之法非海口以待洋寇之術也蓋陸戰攻中

寓守。守中寓攻。方其守也。出壘以衝其守與攻。竝係壘中之人。故其人衆固不能不多。其壘雖多其壘亦不相障礙。如海口之戰則不然。礮臺之兵。不操礮艘之兵。不在礮臺故礮臺不貴多。而礮艘不厭多也。蓋礮臺多則兵分兵分則用士衆。而左者不能拯右。右者不能救左。幸賊船出于中開。左右之臺。相爲障礙。不能用礮惡在其爲利也。且礮艘置乏。進剿無術。如賊連船於相房閒。以絕我海運何以卻之當是時。縱令內港有百礮臺。亦屬無用。雖欲無不戰而屈不可得也。若乃多備礮艘訓練以時。開戰策應。無所不可。足以襲服洋賊。而制其死命。又何苦而海中以此許多之礮臺爲哉。多事之際。其經費亦甚可惜矣。某地縣令某氏。小有才幹素無學問。見西洋陸戰壘圖。而不知其解。杜撰牽合。以成守海口策。當道亦不深究之。以爲是而施行。予深識其非。廔言之川路司農司農稍信然予言。然而遂弗能救。是亦可慨也。

千羊之皮。不如一狐之腋而千金之裘。又非一狐之皮。今欲爲千金之裘。徵之屠羊之家而可乎。

苟得其心。五州之人皆可得而使也。厚而利之導而舍之。敵開之來問我者。亦爲我用矣。何況我民。

予年二十以後。乃知夫有繫一國。三十以後。乃知有繫天下。四十以後。乃知有繫五世界。

凡五十七條

本章

Main course

省曰録・逐語訳 vs 英訳

Translate word for word vs English translation

象山　号。

子明　字(あざな)。

嘉永甲寅　嘉永七年、この一一月に改元して安政元年となる。なお、本巻の頭注・解説では、通常の用法に従い、こういう場合はすべて安政元年のように表記する。

大星　吉田松陰の密航事件に連坐したことをいう。

筆研　ふでとすずり。

巾笥　きぬばりのはこ。

省　謦　録（安政元年稿）

*象山平大星〈またの名は啓〉*子明氏

嘉永甲寅夏四月、大星は事をもつて獄に下れり。繋にあること七月にして、慾を省みるの余、述ぶるところなくんばあらず。しかれども、獄中には*筆研を禁ずれば、藁を存すること能はざりき。ゆゑに久しくして多くは忘れぬ。すでに出でて、その臆記するところを録し、これを*巾笥に蔵し、もつて子孫に貽す。その挙げてもつて衆に示すがごときは、すなはち吾あに敢へてせんや。

"Record of Conscience"
by
Sakuma Shozan

I was accused of a crime and imprisoned in the summer of 1854. During my seven months in prison, I often wanted to look back over the past and put my thoughts together. However, I was forbidden to write with a pen in prison, and so could not leave any note of these things. As a result, I have forgotten many of them with the passing of time.

After my discharge from prison, I wrote down what thoughts I could remember and put them in a box. They are only to be handed down to my progeny; I have no intention at all of making them known to the world at large.

行ふところの道は、もつて自から安んずべし。得るところの事は、もつて自から楽しむべし。罪の有無は我にあるのみ。外より至るものは、あに憂戚するに足らんや。もし忠信にして譴を受くるをもつて辱となさば、すなはち不義にして富みかつ貴きも、またその栄とするところにあるか。

ここに人ありて、君父の疾病を憂へてこれが薬を求め、幸にしてこれの必ず効あるを知らば、すなはちその品の貴賤、名の美悪を問はず、必ずこれを君父に請ふ。君父その名を悪みて許さずんば、すなはち多方これを謀りて竊かにこれを進むることあらんか、そもそもまた坐ながらにしてその手足を啓くを俟たんか。臣子の至誠惻怛の情、固よりその病患を坐視すべからざれば、すなはち後にその怒に逢はんことを知るといへども、またあに竊かにこれを進めざるを得んや。

人の知るに及ばざるところにして、我独りこれを能くするは、これまた天の寵を荷ふなり。天の寵を荷ふことかくのごとくにして、しかもただ一身の為にのみ計り、天下の為に計らざれば、すなはちその天に負くこと、あにまた大ならずや。

古より忠を懐きて罪を被むるもの、何ぞ限らん。吾は怨むことなし。ただ、なほ為すに及ぶべきの時にして為さざれば、まさに病弊をしてまた救ふべからざるに至らしめんとす。これすなはち悲しむべきのみ。

たとひ予今日に死すとも、天下後世、まさに公論あるべし。予また何をか悔い、何をか恨まん。

憂戚　うれえいたむ。
譴　とがめ。
不義にして『論語』述而「不義而富且貴、於我如浮雲」。
請ふ　薬をのむことをたのむという意味。
多方　種々の方法で。
坐ながらにして　なにもしないでじっとしていて。
手足を啓く　死ぬこと。曾子が死に際に、弟子にわが手足を啓けといったという故事に由来する。『論語』泰伯「曾子有疾、召門弟子曰、啓予足、啓予手」。
惻怛　いたみかなしむこと。
天の寵を荷ふ　天のめぐみをうけている、つまり天賦の才能にめぐまれている。こうした自負心とその反面としての使命感とについては、嘉永三年四月二七日付の三村晴山宛手紙

One should be the judge of one's own behaviour.
It is only we ourselves who can properly savour the result of our own behaviour. Whether guilt exists or not is a matter for ourselves to decide; we need not concern ourselves with guilt imposed from outside. I was punished for holding on to my principles. If this should be considered shameful, it would be the same as honouring the acquisition of wealth through dishonest means. For example, let us suppose that a man is worried about the sickness of his master or his father. He goes in search of a medicine, and finds it. If he deems the medicine effective, he will recommend it to his father or master with no concern for its price, brand, or other such considerations.

But his master or father declines to take the medicine, as he dislikes its name. So then, the man has to choose between drawing up a plan to trick his master or father into taking the medicine, or doing nothing and just waiting for him to die. But the affection of a servant or son will not allow him to just watch and do nothing. The man will trick his master or father into taking the medicine, even though he knows he will be scolded after the event. We know things that others cannot know; we can do things that others cannot do. This has been especially bestowed on us by the grace of heaven. But though we are gifted with such special talents, if we thought of them entirely for our own selfish ends, we would be untrue to the grace of heaven. This would then be the larger guilt. Since ancient times, there have been countless examples of people being punished for their loyalty to a cause. Therefore, I would feel no resentment, even if I were punished for my acts of loyalty. On the other hand, if we leave things to take their own course when we should really act on them, the national crisis will develop into a hopeless situation. This is what we should find most deeply regrettable.
My loyalty will be discussed impartially and supported by future generations with absolute certainty, even if I were to meet my death today. For that reason, I have no complaints or regrets.

身は囹圄にありといへども、心に愧怍なければ、自から方寸の虚明なること、平日に異ならざるを覚ゆ。人心の霊は天地と上下同流し、夷狄・患難の他を累はすを得ざることも、また験すべきなり。ただ、北闈は年八十に満ちて、飲食・坐臥も、予にあらずんば安からず。予が逮繫せられてより、音問通ぜず、動静知らず、その憂慮苦悶はまさに如何すべきや。一念これに及べば、尤も情を為しがたし。しかれども、また理をもって排遣し、心を累はすに至らず。
吾この境を履まずんば、この省覚なし。一跌を経れば一知を長ずとは、はたして虚語にあらず。
振抜・特立するは可なり。激昂・忿戻するは不可なり。
心は走作を戒む。
心に秉といひ操といふも、またこれ時々提撕して、理をもってこれに勝つの謂なり。
吾久しく格物に従事すといへども、内にしては家庭につき、外にしては郷党親朋につき、異時に停調処置して、頗るもって当れりとなせるもの、徐にしてこれを省みれば、往々にして大なる過不及ありて、人の意を満たさざりき。みなこれ工夫いまだ熟せず、故いまだ通徹するを得ざりしゆゑなり。策励せざるべけんや。

囹圄 ろうや。
愧怍 はじること。
方寸の虚明なること こころに妄念がなく、すみきっていること。
人心の霊は… 人の霊は古今を通じて天地と一致しており。
他 人心の霊をさす。
北闈 母。闈は婦女または家族のいるところ。
逮繫 とらえられて獄につながれる。
音問 音信。
排遣 おしのける。感情がみだれる。情を為しがたし 感情がみだれる。
一跌 ひとつのつまずき。

振抜 他人をふりはなす。
特立 衆にぬきんでる。
忿戻 いきどおりさからう。
走作 常軌を逸すること。
心に秉といひ操といふ 本心を守ること。秉も操も「とる」という意。
提撕 本心を振いおこす。
格物 事物の理を究めること。朱子学の根本概念の一つである。→三一一頁
異時 以前。
停調 調停。
世故 世の中のできごと。世事。
策励 はげむ。

Even though my physical self were in prison, I would still be of the same serene mind, because I have done nothing to be ashamed of. The human soul moves with heaven and earth, and foreign aggression cannot disturb or shake it from its foundation. My only worry is that my mother is already advanced in age at 80 years. Without me by her side, she cannot feel at ease whatever she is doing, whether eating or drinking, sitting or sleeping.

Since I was arrested, she has heard no word of what is going on. I wonder how greatly she worries about that, and my heart aches when I think of it. But I use my reason to beat off my mental vacillation, and do not let it disturb me.

I reached my current mental attitude for the first time after my experience in jail. It is true that we learn from our mistakes. Rising to the occasion is good, but not if blood rushes to our head. I am cautious about being blindly impetuous.

We use terms like *hei* or *sou* in connection with the human heart, meaning to control and overcome selfish tendencies by using reason. I have tried to master the truth at the bottom of things for a good while. And until now, I have been flattering myself that I did well when using my reason to deal with my family, internally, and with my kinsmen, friends and relatives externally.

When I reflect on my past conduct, however, there have been many times when I have not given satisfaction due to a lack of consideration for others. This was because my grounding and knowledge are still immature and not sufficiently acquainted with the world. I must try harder.

格物の天地造化におけるは却つて易く、人情世故におけるは却つて難し。吾人はすべからくその易きところに狃れて、その難きところに倦むべからず。己を治むるを行ふの規矩は、すなはち厳ならざるべからず。これ己を治むる身を行ふの規矩は、すなはち厳ならざるべからず。これ己を治むる方なり。人を安んずるは、すなはち自から安んずるゆゑんなり。しからざれば、甚だしき受用なし。予おほよそ書を読むには、すべからく熟読すべし。書巻は携ふることを得ず。書室に端居し、厨子を左右にし、検査せんと欲するところ、手に随つて抽繹すると、全然同じからず。日々黙念して、因りてもつて薬石となし、針砭となすものは、平素に精読し暗記するところのものに過ぎず。少き時には専ら博渉を務め、多く群書を読みしが、率ねみな存するがごとく、亡するがごとくにして、今、記し起さんと欲すれども、卒に能はざれば、多しといへども、またなんぞもつてなさん。他日幸に放還せらるるを得ば、まさにもつて後生に諗げ、かつもつて自から警むべきなり。

予ここに来りしより、勉励克治して、身心を鍛錬し、いまだ嘗て虚しく時日を度らず。古人云へらく、もし間居すとも、真に空しく日月を過さずんば、かの我を鋼ぐものは、みな我を成すなりと。旨あるかな。

造化　自然。

人を待つ　人を待遇する。人をあつかう。

受用　身につけ実践に役立てること。

端居　平生の意であるが、正坐して生活するという意に用いたものか。

厨子　本箱。

抽繹　ぬきだす。

薬石　わが身のいましめにするもの。石は石針で古代の医療器具。

針砭　医療のはり。針はかねのはり、砭は石のはり。

博渉　ひろく書物をみること。

後生　後進の人々。

克治　私欲にかち邪念を治める。

間居　仕事なくひまでいる。『大学』に「小人間居為二不善一」とある。

Finding the truth at the bottom of things is difficult in the human world, though it is relatively easy in the natural world. We must not become too accustomed to easy things and avoid difficult ones. Our model of self-behaviour should be strict. This is a principle of self-management, and if we can keep self-control, then we can manage others too. But we should not be too strict when dealing with others. This is the principle for satisfying others; if others can be satisfied, then we ourselves can be satisfied too.

When reading a book, we should read it so closely that we can recite it. Otherwise it will not be so rewarding.
When I was in prison, I had no books by my side. To be able to sit in my study with books on either side and take one out when it pleases me is quite a different environment. But in jail, I did nothing but think in silence day by day.

The only thing that helped and admonished my thoughts in jail at that time was my memorization based on reading books diligently day by day.
In my younger days, I read so many books to extend my knowledge, but it was as if I remembered them and forgot them at the same time. Consequently, if someone had made me write everything word for word, I would not have been able to. Therefore, it is not necessarily always beneficial to read a lot of books. If I am acquitted and enjoy my freedom by some happy chance, I must teach this to younger people, and must also admonish myself.

After entering the prison, I wasted not a single day, but strove for physical and mental training, as well as studying hard based on self-control. As someone said long ago, "I may be forced to live in seclusion, but as long as I waste no time, the one who locks me away will actually help me to grow". This is exactly correct.

門葉　一門。一族。
飽暖　飽食暖衣の略、衣食にこと欠かないこと。
牢錬　厳しい鍛錬をする。
緩急　危急の事変。
弥利堅　米国。
江都　江戸。
恬然　平気でいる。
重囚　重罪人。
麁食　粗食。
転側　ねがえりをうつ。
支体　身体。
外邪　やまい、やまいは外から人身をおそってくるという考えに基づく。
心志　こころざし。
多子　多くの条件。
津　つば。

予、門葉衰薄なりといへども、いまだ寒苦の境に*牢錬するを経ず。常に恐らくは、一旦国家に緩急あらば、起居飲食、多くは勝へざるところあらんと。しかるに、去夏*弥利堅の舶突かに至りて、*江都戒厳せしとき、予、藩邸の為に軍務を経理し、睡ることを得ざるもの七昼夜なりしも、精神ますます奮ひぬ。今歳罪を得獄に下り、*麁食を飯ひ塩を嚙み、*重囚と伍をなすこと数旬なりしも、*恬然としてこれに安んじ、精神活潑にして、身もまた健康なり。この二事は少しく自から試験し、益を得たること細ならず。また天の賜といふべし。

*外邪の人を襲ふは、多くは睡眠の時にあり。ゆゑに中夜寝に就くも、熟眠するを得ず。速かに寤めしめんが為には、常にまさに意を係けて醒にあるべし。もし支体に安からざるところあらば、或いは手をもってこれを摩し、或いは随意に*転側し、務めて血気をして停滞するところなからしむ。もし咽喉滑かならずんば、或いは舌を運らして*津を嚥み、或いは息を深くして気を閉ぢ、少焉にしてこれを放つ。かくのごとくこれを行はば、外邪もまた侵すことを得ず。

内には*心志を定め、外には血気を運らし、昼には飲食を節し、夜には睡眠を少くす。脩養の妙訣は果して*多子なし。

Although my family had been in decline, I wanted for nothing in life and had never known true hardship. As a result, I had always doubted whether I could withstand inconveniences of food, clothing and shelter in a state of national emergency.

When the American warships suddenly arrived last summer, martial law was proclaimed in Edo. I performed my military duties in the residential estate of the feudal domain, and grew increasingly spirited, despite going without sleep for seven consecutive nights. But I was accused of a crime and put in jail this year. Since then, I have been forced to live with felons for many days and nights, eating plain food and gnawing on salt. In spite of that, my condition is healthy, my spirits are high and I suffer no hardship.

    I have obtained great benefit and tested myself through these two experiences. They should be seen as blessings from heaven.

Malicious spirits from outside often possess the bodies of human beings as they sleep. When we go to bed at night, we must never fall into a deep sleep. We should always be able to call our consciousness to attention, so that we can wake up immediately.

If you feel uneasy about your physical condition, try to improve your circulation by rubbing your body with your hands or changing your sleeping position in bed. And if you get something stuck in your throat, swallow saliva by moving your tongue, breathe deeply then hold your breath, and then exhale again after a little while. Do this, and the malicious spirit cannot infiltrate. Be emotionally stable inside but passionate on the outside, take appropriate meals in the daytime, and sleep in moderation at night. These are the conditions for self-discipline; other detailed instructions should not be necessary.

勢賀　伊勢と伊賀。
衙署　やくしょ。
駅亭　しゅくば。
傾塌　かたむきたおれる。
丁未　弘化四年（一八四七）。
揺撼　ゆれうごく。
清人の雑書　底本の頭注に、「張泓所ㇾ著滇南新語」とある。
蚕叢　荒地。
漢儒　漢代の儒者。後述のような思想は『漢書』五行志などに多く見えている。
侵陵　おかしあなどる。
占候　自然現象で吉凶をうらなうこと。
天人合応の理　天地自然の現象と人間社会の現象とがたがいに感応するという理法。漢代に盛んになった天人相関思想であり、後世の儒教にも残存した。

聞く、関西、地震ひ、勢賀の間、さらに甚だしく、城垣衙署、駅亭民屋、傾塌すること算なく、樹木倒植し、井水乾涸し、人民圧死すること、ほとんどその数を知らずと。丁未に信州の地大いに震ひしとき、予郷里にありて、親しくその変を閲せしが、惨毒の劇しきこと、言ふに忍びざるところなりき。信中の変後には、地下毎に雷声を作し、時にまた揺撼し、久しきを経るも止まず。後七年にして今また関西の変あり。嘗て清人の雑書載するところを記するに、云ふ、その地常に動かば、数年の後に至りて大震あり、万家の楽土、忽ち蚕叢に変ずと。しからばすなはち、地震には固より数年に連なるものあり。古来漢儒は地震をもつて蛮夷が侵陵するの兆となせり。占候の説は洋学の取らざるところなり。しかりといへども、天人合応の理は、必ずこれなしとは謂ふべからず。丁未以来の地震の変をば、時事をもつてこれを験するに、いま夷虜の志はいまだその極まるところを知らざれば、すなはち震の相連なりて、なほ劇甚なるものあらんも、また慮ることなき能はず。

Word has spread that there was an earthquake in the Kansai area, and the areas around Iga and Ise were particularly devastated. The earthquake brought everything down, including castle walls, public offices, post stations and private houses. They say it uprooted trees and dried up wells, while countless people were crushed to death.
There was a huge earthquake in Shinshu Province in 1847. I inspected the damage when I stayed in my hometown at that time, but could find no words to express such a tragic event.

After that, the situation continued for a long time with tremors and vibrations whenever something happened. And then, the Odawara earthquake finally occurred seven years later in 1853, followed by the Kansai earthquake in the very next year. A book written by someone in the Qing Dynasty stated that a huge earthquake would occur several years later if the land was constantly moving; Mother Earth, so crowded with people in densely built-up areas, would soon be a wasteland, like the silkworm bed made famous in a poem by Li Bai. In that case, there must be some earthquakes that continue for several years by nature.

Confucians in ancient China considered earthquakes to be a premonition that "barbarians" would invade. Although western learning pays no heed to divination, we cannot state categorically that there is no correspondence between the natural and human worlds. When we consider the earthquakes that have occurred since 1847 and happenings in the human world, there is no reason to negate the theory proposed by the Confucians. Judging from appearances, the aspirations of foreign powers appear to be strengthening limitlessly, while on the other hand, violent earthquakes like this still continue. Things may grow even harsher in the near future, in terms of both natural movements and secular problems.

[＊関西の地震は六月十四日にありて、獄中にこれを伝ふるは二十四、五日の間にあり。季秋に放還せられし後に、この録を次第せしが、十一月四日に至りて、東海道の地、また大いに震ひ、城郭を隳り廬舎を壊り、死傷無数なりき。因りて竊かに書して江都の所親に寄せ、告ぐるにこの条の大意をもってし、都下も恐らくはまた免れずと謂ひて、これをして平素に戒備するところあらしめき。明年十月二日の夜、江都に果して大震ありて、火またこれに従ふ。その余烈はこの前の数災に比するに、超過すること数倍なり。しかれども予が旧より親交するところは、多くはこれを保全するを得たり。これ天意なりといへども、また小しく予が言に資ることなくんばあらず。乙卯の冬に記す。]

関西の地震は… 以下、底本は頭注。

季秋　晩秋。象山が在所において蟄居すべしという判決をうけたのは九月一八日で、江戸を発ったのは九月二五日である。

次第　順序だてる。整理する。

廬舎　いえ。

所親　親しい人。

戒備　用心し備える。

余烈　あとまで残るわざわい。

資る　もちいる。

乙卯　安政二年（一八五五）。

The Kansai earthquake occurred on July 9th, but I only knew of it ten or eleven days later.
I wrote this description after leaving jail in September, and then another earthquake occurred throughout Tokaido on December 23rd. Castles were destroyed, private houses collapsed, and countless lives were lost.

I then wrote letters to my relatives and friends in Edo to give them an outline of these events. I said they should make preparations, as an earthquake was also sure to occur in Edo. In fact, the earthquake occurred the following year, on the night of November 11th, 1855. Fires broke out and the damage was several times greater than in so many past earthquakes.

However, my acquaintances were mostly unaffected by it. That they remained safe must be due to providence, but there is no doubt that my prediction also contributed a little. (Postscript: winter of 1855.)

君子に五の楽しみあり。しかうして、富貴は与からず。一門礼義を知りて、骨肉釁隙なきは、一の楽なり。取予苟くもせず、廉潔自から養ひ、心に大道を識り、内には妻孥に愧ぢず、外には衆民に怍ぢざるは、二の楽なり。聖学を講明し、時に随ひ義に安んじ、険に処ること夷のごときは、三の楽なり。西人が理窟を啓くの後に生れて、古の聖賢のいまだ嘗て識らざるところの理を知るは、四の楽なり。東洋道徳、西洋芸術、精粗遺さず、表裏兼該し、因りてもつて民物を沢くし、国恩に報ゆるは、五の楽なり。孔聖の浮雲の志を抗げ、鄒叟の浩然の気を養ひ、寵辱驚かず、困極にありといへども、天地の際を究め、古今の変を観、万物の理を玩び、人身の紀を稽ぶれば、饑ゑて食ひ、渇して飲み、坐して思ひ、倦みて睡り、逌然として自得し、また身の圜牆の中にあるを知らず。

のであろう。『孟子』尽心上「君子有三楽、而王三天下、不二与存一焉、父母俱存、兄弟無レ故、一楽也、仰不レ愧二於天一、俯不レ怍二於人一、二楽也、得二天下英才一、而教二育之一、三楽也」。富貴は…五つの楽しみの中に富貴ははいっていないとまずいい、その後で五つの楽しみを順次のべているわけである。

釁隙　なかたがい。

取予　うけとることとあたえること。

妻孥　妻と子、家人。

義に安んじ　楽しんで義をふみ行う。

夷　平坦。

精粗遺さず　こまかい点も大まかな点も、きわめつくす。

兼該　かねそなえる。

民物を沢し　人々に恩恵を与える。

浮雲の志を抗げ　はかない不義の富貴をにくむ志を昂揚させる。『論語』述而「飯二疏食一飲レ水、曲レ肱而枕レ之、楽亦在二其中一矣。不義而富且貴、於レ我如二浮雲一」。

鄒叟　孟子。鄒国（孟子の生国）の老人の意。

浩然の気　天地間に充満している正大な元気。『孟子』公孫丑上「我善養二吾浩然之気一…其為レ気也、至大至剛以直、養而無レ害、則塞二于天地之間二」。

寵辱　ほめられることとそしられること。

俛仰怍ぢず　仰いでは天にたいし、俯しては地にたいしてやましいことがない。

紀　すじ、条理。

逌然　くつろぐさま。

圜牆　ろうや。

A man of virtue has five pleasures, but they are not related to property or status.

The first pleasure is that one's whole family observes proprieties and does not become estranged from parent-child or brother-sister relationships.

The second pleasure is to do nothing by halves when giving or receiving money and goods, to live an honest life and be true internally to one's wife and child, and externally to society at large.

The third is to study the teachings of the sages, to be aware of nature and human righteousness, and to be able to treat a crisis in the same way as a normal situation, with a sense of justice in conformity with the times.

The fourth is to grasp things that even Confucius and Mencius never knew, which have come into being since westerners evolved natural sciences.

And the fifth pleasure is to study both Eastern ethics and Western technical learning precisely and completely, and then to make these serve the state and contribute to people's lives.

Confucius shunned transitory, unstable wealth and fame, which he likened to the movement of clouds. Mencius also discharged his duties in a broad-minded spirit without being burdened by worldly affairs. I too want to behave like this. I will firmly reject patronage and insult, and will always aim to avoid casting shame on others through my behaviour. And I will consider all things until the end of the earth, and observe how things have changed between ancient and modern. Then, when I have learnt about all things in creation, then apply that knowledge and consider patterns of human behaviour, I will be able to find pleasure in that, even though I may face the most extreme hardship.
Eat if hungry, drink if thirsty, think while seated, and sleep if tired. If I could reach a composed mental state like that, I could even forget that I was in jail.

敏の一字は、これ学を為すの法にして、治を為すの要も、またこれに若くはなし。天下の学ぶべく為すべきの務は、このごとくそれ広く、かのごとくそれ大なり。ゆゑに学と治とは、みなもつて敏ならざるべからず。かの身を学に終へて、空疎にして用なく、身を官に終へて、因循にして功なきものは、その力を勤むること敏ならざるに坐すること、十のうち常に八、九なり。

孔子の聖も、なほかつ憤りを発して食を忘れ、敏にしてもつてこれを求めたり。何ぞいはんや吾が輩をや。

日晷一たび移れば、千載に再来の今なく、形神すでに離るれば、万古に再生の我なし。学芸・事業は、あに悠々たるべけんや。

蓋し男子が身を立つるの第一義なり。しかれどもその初は、専ら防禦の為にして設けたり。防禦ことは、射に礼射・武射の別あり。ゆゑにその生るや、桑の弧蓬の矢、もつて天地四方を射て、しかる後に敢へて穀を用ふるも、また第一義を示すなり。男子今の世に生れて、弓矢長兵はみなその利たるを失へり。銃礟を知らざるは、それ可ならんや。その初生においても、またよろしく礟をもつて弧矢に換へ、上下四方に発して、もつてその事あるところに志すべきなり。

敏 つとめること。『論語』述而「我非三生而知之者一、好レ古敏以求レ之者也」。

因仍 因循姑息。

憤りを発して…『論語』述而「其為レ人也、発憤忘レ食、楽以忘レ憂、不レ知二老之将レ至一也云爾」。

日晷 光陰。

形神 肉体と精神。

その生るや…『礼記』射義「男子生るるや、桑の弧、蓬の矢六つ、以て天地四方は射る。天地四方は男子の事ある所なり。故に必ず先づその事ある所に志すことありて、しかる後に敢へて穀を用ふ、飯食するの謂なり」。

長兵 長い武器、槍やなぎなた。

礟 砲と同じ。

The Japanese word *bin*, meaning "be quick to seize opportunity", is both a basis for study and is also unsurpassed as a political keyword. There are very many things to do and study in the world. Therefore we must be *bin* – quick to seize opportunity – whether in our studies or when engaged in politics.

For instance, there are some people in the world who learn for the sake of learning and live out their lives uselessly by cramming knowledge into their heads. On the other hand, there are others who have no merit, in spite of holding government posts. This is because they are not *bin*, and so their efforts yield no results. Out of every ten people, eight or nine are like this.

Even a sage like Confucius aspired to *bin*, forgetting personal needs in his resolve to make those efforts. This should apply all the more to a person like me.

As one day follows the other, today will never return, even though thousands of years may go by. When I am dead and my spirit is separated from my physical self, I will never be reborn even though thousands of years may go by. For this reason, I cannot move slowly, whether in the field of study or in that of business. When a man shoots an arrow, there is a difference between shooting as part of a ceremony and shooting in a war. Originally, however, bows were only designed for defence. Defence is the most important thing of all when a man goes out into the world. That's why we have a ceremony when a boy is born, in which mugwort arrows are shot in all directions from a mulberry bow; only then is the baby deemed ready to enter the world of manhood. This indicates that defence is the most important issue.

In this respect, the advantage of bows, arrows and spears has been lost, due to the use of guns. Boys today cannot enter manhood without knowledge of guns. So if a baby boy is born, a cannon should be fired in all directions instead of the mulberry bow, to show the strength of his resolve to join the world.

原　源と同じ。特異な意見の発端の意か。
　君相　君と大臣と。
　積累　つみかさねること。この言葉は格物致知との関連において、宋学で頻用されている。
　素　素地、したじ。
　耳を提げてこれに告ぐ　こんこんとさとす。「提耳面命」という言葉がある。
　易侮　あなどること。易もあなどるの意。
　防堵　台場（だい）。堵はかき。
　式　方式、きまり。
　接するところの　外国と折衝するところの。
　甲兵　軍備。
　本根を託す　国防という基礎を置く。
　果決　思いきって行うこと。
　糜がん　とりおさえよう。
　啓きて　てびきして。
　従容　慫慂、すすめ誘う。
　捍禦　ふせぎまもること。
　文具　かざりもの。
　一塗　ひとすじ、一途。

　予久しく意を海防に留む。その発明するところは、自から謂へらく、前人はいまだ及ばざるものありと。しかれども卒にこれによりて禍を取れるは、また非常の*原は、常人これを異しむのみ。*君相もし省悟するの時あらば、すなはち吾が志の行はれんこと、必せり。
　おほよそ学問は、必ず*積累をもつてす。一朝一夕の能く通暁するにあらず。海防の利害も、またこれ一大学問なり。講究すること*素あるものにあらざるよりは、いまだ遽かにその要領を得やすからず。人、*耳を提げてこれに告ぐといへども、しかも解せざるは、蓋しまたこれに由る。
　外夷をして易侮の心を開かしめざるは、これ防禦の至要なり。辺海の*防堵は、みなその法を得ず。陳ぬるところの銃器は、みなその*式に中らず。接するところの官吏は、みな凡夫庸人にして、胸に*甲兵なし。かくのごとくにして、夷人の侮心を開くことなからんことを欲するも、寧んぞ得べけんや。
　敵国外患ありて、しかも*本根を託することいまだ固からず。形勢いまだならず、進んでは*果決の勇なく、退きては遷延の計を持するものは、その敵を*糜がんと欲するはまさにもつて敵を啓きて自から糜ぐに足り、その寇を緩めんと欲するところのものも、またまさに*寇に資して自から緩むに足る。その*従容・補綴してその捍禦の備を全くせんと欲するところの勢はいよいよ支ふべからざるに至る。しかるに古来、局に当るもの、曾て深く省みず、家国天下を誤ること、*一塗に出づるがごとし。歎ずるに勝ふべけんや。

Thanks to my lengthy study of naval defence, I feel proud to have gained more excellent ideas than my seniors. Ironically, though, I became a transgressor as a result of this. My thoughts are not understood by normal people, because they go beyond common knowledge. But when the statesmen realize their error, my ideas will be put into practice for sure.   Broadly speaking, study has to be accumulated step by step, and therefore cannot be completed in the space of a day. Knowing the advantages and disadvantages of naval defence is also a major study. Unless a man studies hard, based on knowledge about this, he will not be able to follow its content. This is why a man who only has the intention to hear but does not attempt to master will not understand, even if one were to explain the core issues of naval defence.   The most important thing about naval defence is not to generate derision among foreigners. On the other hand, the system for defending our coasts is not fit for purpose, while the small arms laid out there are being used erroneously. Furthermore, the government employees who are in contact with the foreigners are mediocre people; they do not hold a great determination in their hearts. If this situation continues, it is inevitable that the foreigners will look down on us. The state policy is still defined without basic countermeasures for that and the defence system is still not completed, even though we are at risk of invasion by a foreign enemy. In some cases, simply adopting delaying tactics without engaging in battle can only serve to restrict oneself; it is really like untying the enemy's hands, instead of binding them up. And it unfastens the unity of our supporters, since it gives power to the enemy instead of undoing the enemy's offensive.

Even if one government official happened to plan a national system and prepare defence installations calmly in this period, it would merely be an empty gesture when overall circumstances are like this. Japan's national system has collapsed, and the severity of this will merely accelerate. When faced with such a situation, government officials run headlong toward demise

膏粱 美食。あぶらののった肉とおいしい飯。

師律 軍律。

衝突 勢い鋭く攻めてくること。

故家世族 ふるくから続いている家と代々ろくをうける家

義会 義勇団。

校試稽攷 考査する。

韜略 兵法、軍略。六韜・三略の省略。

謀獻 はかりごと。ここでは、韜略を戦術、謀獻を戦略、もしくは前者を純軍事的なはかりごと、後者をより政治的なはかりごと、という意味で用いているのであろう。

統馭 統率。

警急 危急のできごと。非常事態。

鳩集 あつめあわせる。

師陣 軍隊。

陣 陣だて。

呉子 呉起、戦国時代の衛の人、曾子に学び、用兵に秀でていた。魯・魏・楚に仕えた。兵書『呉子』はその著作と伝えられる。下の引用はその図国篇にでている。

警省 用心して反省する。

今の将帥の任に当るものは、公侯貴人にあらずんば、すなはち*膏粱の氏族にして、平日飲酒歌舞をもつて娯しみとなし、兵謀*師律の何事たるかを知らず。一旦国家の急あらば、誰か能く軍士の服することなりて、敵人の*衝突を遏めんや。これ今の深患なり。ゆゑに予嘗て西洋武備の大略に倣ひ、天下の兵籍の外において、*故家世族の忠勇剛毅にして、一も*義会となし、*もつて義会となして十に当るべきものを結び、もつて志となさんと欲す。その初め会に入らんとするや、*校試稽攷し、果して艱苦を憚らざれば、まさに始めて入ることを聴す。*韜略、*謀獻、*統馭の才あるものを推して、これが長となし、*警急の日に遇はば、すなはち*鳩集して師を成し、もつて官の指揮を待たしめん。庶はくは、寇を攘ひ勲を植つること、或いは兵籍にあるものの上に居らんことを。

戦の必ず勝たんことを欲せば、陣の必ず定まるにあらずんば不可なり。守の必ず固きにあらずんば不可なり。魏侯、陣の必ず定まるの道を問ひしに、呉子曰く、「君能く賢者をして上に居り、不肖者をして下に処らしめば、すなはち陣すでに定まる」と。今、天下の諸国、賢者いまだ必ずしも上に居らず、不肖者いまだ必しも下に処らず。しからばすなはち、陣いまだ定まらざるなり。陣いまだ定まらざるに、その守必ず固く、戦必ず勝つものは、いまだこれあらざるなり。志あるの主よ、尚はくはそれ*警省するところを知らんことを。

without deep introspection, as was always the case. This is indeed a matter for regret.

The current army leaders are appointed to managerial positions merely by reason of their high status or their family background; they have almost no knowledge of war tactics or strategy. Their daily lives are spent in pleasures like amusement and drinking. With people like that, it will be impossible to fend off an enemy attack and take command of the army when a national emergency occurs. For the time being, this is the most significant issue. Therefore, my previous plan was to assist the national security and protect the people by creating a company of voluntary comrades, imitating the western army system. The company would comprise devoted men of stouthearted character, each of whom would be as good as ten others. When admitting men to the company, only those who passed the qualifying examination to prove that they could overcome difficulties and pains would be permitted. And then my plan was to select a talented person as leader, then gather them quickly and activate them under government command in the event of an emergency. If there were such an organization, it could surely be expected to render more distinguished service to the state than government army specialists when it came to eliminating an external enemy. If the state truly wishes to win a war, it must first strengthen its defence against enemy attack. And to strengthen its defence, it would need to establish a wartime footing. In olden times, when the Lord of Wei in China asked how he should establish a wartime footing, Wu Qi answered that such a footing would naturally be established if the wise were set on top and the unworthy were set below them. In Japan today, the principle of setting the wise on top and the unworthy below them is not always observed, even in the armies of each feudal domain of the Tokugawa Shogunate. As a result, a wartime footing has not been established.

教練精ならず、賞罰明かならず、また能くこれを用ふるものなくんば、たとひ億万の衆ありとも、その戦・守におけるは、いはゆる*伏鶏・乳犬のみ。その貍と虎とを如何せんや。
「*力を同じくすれば徳を度り、徳を同じくすれば義を量る」。文王の美を称すといへども、また、「*大国はその力を畏れ、小国はその徳に懐く」といふに過ぎず。その力なくして能くその国を保つものは、古より今に至るまで、吾いまだこれを見ざるなり。誰か王者は力を尚ばずといふか。

*彼を知らず、己を知るも、今の時にありては、戦ふごとに必ず敗るるは、固よりなり。悉く彼の善くするところを善くして、しかも己の能くするところを喪はずして、しかる後に始めてもつて戦を言ふべし。

*詳証術は万学の基本なり。泰西この術を発明し、兵略もまた大いに進み、*貪然として往時と別なり。いはゆる*下学して上達するなり。孫子の兵法の度・量・数・称・勝も、またその術なり。しかれども漢と我とは、孫子ありて以来、*誦習して講説せざることなくして、その兵法は依然として旧のごとく、泰西と比肩するを得ず。これ他なし、下学の功なきに坐するなり。今真に武備を*脩飭せんと欲せば、先づこの学科を興すにあらずんば、不可なり。

伏鶏・乳犬 卵を抱いたにわとりと子を育てつつある犬。『呉子』巻首に「譬へば、なほ伏鶏の貍を搏ち、乳犬の虎を犯すがごとく、闘心ありといへども、これに随はば死せん」とある。
力を同じくすれば… 『書経』泰誓にある周の武王の言葉。ただし原文では「同力度徳、同徳度義」となっている。
文王 周王朝をひらいた武王の父。聖人君主として名高い。
大国は… 『書経』武成にある周の武王の言葉。
彼を知らず… 『孫子』謀攻篇「知彼知己、百戦不殆。…不知彼不知己、毎戦必殆」。
度・量・数・称・勝 『孫子』軍形篇。土地の広さや距離を度り、人口や糧食を量り、兵数を数え、敵と比較することを通して、勝をおさめることをいう。
詳証術 オランダ語のウィスキュンデ wiskunde の訳、数学のこと。
貪然 はるかに。
下学して上達 手近い所から次第に深い学問へ進む。『論語』憲問「不怨天、不尤人、下学而上達」。
誦習 読んでならう。
脩飭 おさめととのえる。

A wartime footing has not been established, and moreover the nation has no experience of winning through stout defence. I hope sensible rulers will think well over this point.

Training is imperfect, rewards and punishments are unreasonable, and there is nobody with the ability to command. Under such conditions, even with a countless number of soldiers, it would be like a chicken sitting on an egg or a dog leading its suckling puppy. How can we face up squarely to a strong enemy like a cunning racoon dog or a tough tiger? It is said that superiority and inferiority in terms of virtue can only be measured when power is equal, and the same goes for morality when power and virtue are identical. Furthermore, even when the virtue of King Wen of the Zhou Dynasty is praised, in reality it is merely that "large nations feared his power, while small nations were swayed by his virtue." I have heard of no case, in either ancient or modern times, in which a state has maintained its system without power. Kings should respect power. A nation will definitely lose a war if it knows not its own power nor that of its enemy. But under the current situation, it would still not be enough to know both one's own power and that of one's opponent. One can only expect to win a war when one is able to maintain one's advantage but also fully absorb the opponent's advantage. Mathematics is the basis of all forms of study. Western nations have greatly evolved their military strategies thanks to their development of mathematics. As a result, they are quite different from what they once were. They have made rapid progress by consolidating their foundations.

In *The Art of War*, Sun Tzu referred to the five articles of weights, measures, numbers, names and victories, thus indicating the importance of mathematics. But although this idea has been broadcast loudly in China and Japan since Sun Tzu, no progress has been made in military learning, and we now lag far behind the West.

＊士大夫は、必ず人に過ぎたるの胆量ありて、まさに能く戎狄の気を奪ひて、本国の威を伸ぶ。＊郭汾陽の単騎にして虜を見るがごとき、能く戎狄の辞を屈して、本国の体を存す。必ず人に過ぎたるの学問才弁ありて、能く戎狄の辞を屈して、本国の体を存す。＊富文忠の献納の二字を却けたるがごときは、これなり。今□天朝の＊縉紳にして、しばしば夷使と接するものは、果して汾陽の胆量あるか、果して文忠の学問才弁あるか。吾、竊かにこれを危ぶむ。人はその畏るべきを見ずんば、すなはち必ずこれを慢易す。一たびその慢易の心を啓かば、また何をもってか能くこれを治めんや。ゆゑに君子は必ずこれに臨むに荘をもってす。＊その衣冠を正しくし、その＊瞻視を尊くし、＊辞気を出すにここに鄙倍に遠ざかるは、みな荘をなすゆゑんの方なり。今の士大夫は、往々、＊挙措軽佻、言辞げ鄙猥にして、もつて自から人を服せしむること難し。ああ、人情に通じて人を喜ぶものあり。その意は、蓋し謂へらく、かくのごとくならざれば、もつて人情に通じて人を服せしむるものは、自からその道あるあり。今その道をもつてせずして、この醜態を露さば、吾恐らくは、その人を服せしめんと欲するものは、まさにもつてその慢易を導くに足らんことを。

士大夫 中国では、周代に天子や諸侯に仕えるもののうち、上級のものを大夫、下級のものを士といった。ここでは官に仕えているものをさす。江戸時代の支配層は本来武士であり、中国のごとき文治官僚とはかなり性格が異なるが、江戸時代にはこの相違がほとんど無視され、武士を士大夫と称していた。

郭汾陽 唐の将軍郭子儀。安禄山の乱の鎮圧につくした。その後、懐恩・吐蕃・回紇の連合軍が侵入した際には、回紇を懐柔することによって吐蕃を破り唐朝の危機を救った。

体 体面。

富文忠 北宋の政治家富弼。契丹・西夏との外交折衝を担当した。契丹が関南の地の割譲を求めた折に、割譲を拒み、歳幣を増すことによって交戦の危機を救った。

縉紳 高位高官。

慢易 あなどる。

荘 威儀があり荘重なこと。『論語』為政「臨」之以」荘則敬」。

その衣冠を… 『論語』堯曰「君子正二其衣冠一、尊二其瞻視一」。瞻視はめつき。

辞気を出すに… 『論語』泰伯「出二辞気一、斯遠二鄙倍一矣」。鄙倍は鄙俗で理にそむくこと。

挙措 ふるまい。

This is what I want to say to you. It is because we did not consolidate the foundations of sciences and military study based on mathematical evolution. If someone were really to provide military equipment now, mathematics would have to be elevated first of all.   The "scholar-officials" who served the Chinese dynasties had extraordinary courage and generosity. They raised China's prestige through overwhelming victories over border tribes (known as barbarians) in all directions. (Note: "Scholar-officials" were individuals who combined the roles of bureaucrats, landlords and men of letters, from the Northern Song Dynasty onwards.) A good example is Guo Fenyang, whose original name was Guo Ziyi (697-781). He is said to have ridden alone to meet a group of captives and gained their allegiance by the very power of his presence. What's more, scholar-officials had greater learning and eloquence than normal people, and maintained the appearance of the state by rejecting the demands of the barbarians from all directions. Fu Wenzhong's rejection of a demand for tribute, and his ultimate success in obtaining a monetary settlement instead, is a good example of this.

Today, I wonder whether Japanese government officials would display Guo Fenyang's generosity when contacting outlanders' delegations. I wonder whether they have Fu Wenzhong's learning and eloquence. I am swayed by misgivings, privately.

The people will hold a statesman in absolute contempt if they meet him and do not recognize the need to respect him. And once such contempt occurs, the statesman will be unable to rule over them. This is why, whenever a ruler comes into contact with the people, he always behaves with correct manners. Thus, for example, the ruler wears formal court dress properly, behaves with due courtesy and attention to the expressions used when talking with others, and does not come out with vulgar or unreasonable words. These examples explain how a ruler should behave when in contact with the people.

Today, however, there are some civil servants who take delight in

人の己を誉むるも、己において何をか加へん。もし誉によりて自から怠らば、すなはち反つて損せん。人の己を毀るも、己において何をか損せん。もし毀によりて自から強めば、反つて益せん。

＊人の過あり、事の過あり。人の過は、もつて人を観るべし。

事の過は、いまだもつて人を観るべからず、人の過は、もつて人を観るべし。

今のいはゆる儒者は、果して何するものぞや。本朝＊神聖造国の道、＊堯舜三代帝王の治は、兼ねて明かにしてこれを＊黙識するか。礼楽刑政、典章制度より、もつて兵法・師律・械器の利に至るまで、講論してみなその要を得たるか。土境の形勢、海陸道路の＊険夷、外蕃の情状、＊防戍の利害、城堡・＊堵堞・＊控援の略、推算・重力・幾何・詳証の術、並びに究めてこれを悉すか。吾いまだこれを知らざるなり。しからばすなはち、今のいはゆる儒者は、果して何するものぞや。

書を読み学を講ずるに、徒らに空言をなして当世の務に及ばざれば、＊清談して事を廃すると＊一間のみ。

＊有用の学は、譬へば夏時の＊葛、冬時の＊裘のごとし。もしこれを為るものなくんば、すなはち＊生民の用闕けん。

これあるも補ふところなく、これなきも損するところなきは、すなはち無用の学なり。

人の過　人の本質にかかわるようなあやまち。

造国　建国。

堯舜三代　堯舜と夏・殷・周の三代、儒教では理想的な政治が行われていた時代とされる。

黙識　心の中におぼえこむ。

険夷　けわしいとたいらかと。

防戍　防衛。

堵堞　防塁。

控援　統率。

一間　わずかなへだたり。

清談　俗ばなれしたはなし。

葛　くずの繊維で作ったかたびら。

裘　毛皮で作ったころも。

生民　たみ、人民。

rough speech and rash action. It seems they are convinced that they cannot win the devotion of the people through human sentiment without doing that. This is not acceptable.

There are ways of winning the devotion of the people through human sentiment. Civil servants make a terrible mistake by not using these ways but behaving disgracefully, with the result that they win the people's contempt when they intended to win their devotion. I worry about this. Even if others speak well of me, what do I really gain by it? If I obtain praise and am then neglectful, I incur a greater loss. On the other hand, even if others criticize me, I suffer not the slightest loss. If their criticism stimulates me to make efforts, if anything it will be to my benefit. There are two types of fault, one caused by human error and another for which no one is responsible. Therefore, we should not judge a person on the basis of accidents. Only when a person is responsible for a fault are there grounds to judge that person. Just what are today's Confucian scholars doing? I really wonder whether they have understood or assimilated the great principle of Japan's founding as a sacred nation and the policy of rule by the Yao Shun three Emperors of ancient China. I wonder whether they grasp the points of military strategy based on politics with systems of commendation and punishment. And does their discussion extend as far as military discipline, or even the utilization of mechanical equipment and devices?
I wonder whether they rigorously study everything regarding topographical forms, the difficulty of routes between sea and land, the circumstances of the enemy, advantages and disadvantages in defending against that enemy, how to build castles and fortresses, the arrangement of reinforcements, and so on, as well as continuing to study physics and mathematics. I have never heard of such a person. Just what are today's Confucian scholars doing, if that is so? People may read books and study, but if that alone has no use in their actual work, they are almost the same

百姓　人民。

凍餒　こごえうえ。

飽逸　たらふく飲食をし、たのしみにふける。

貧窶　まずしいこと。

百姓足らば…　『論語』顔淵。

本邦の…　勝海舟宛書簡

浩　あてる、用いる。

宴饗　酒盛をしてもてなすこと。

劣済困窮の家　家計のやりくりがつかず困窮している家。

飼糧購賞の費　兵糧と論功行賞の費用。

応接給資の用　外交に用いる費用。

本邦の金貨米粟は…

莫大。

　帝王の政は、財を民に蔵して、余あれば取り、足らざれば与ふ。ゆゑに百姓を凍餒せしめて、上独り富足せず、また百姓を飽逸せしめて、国独り貧窶ならず。ゆゑに曰く、「百姓足らば、君孰れとともにか足らざらん、百姓足らずんば、君孰れとともにか足らん」と。これ天下古今不易の道なり。

　本邦の金貨米粟は、号して富饒と為す。しかれども疆域大ならず。ゆゑに邦内に生ずるところの財をもって、邦内に為すところの用に享すれば、甚だしくは有余なし。すなはち海防の事のごときは、すなはち外に起るものなり。防堵を置くこと数百所、大艦を造ること数百艘、巨礮を鋳ること数千門なれば、その費もまた浩なり。しかも、みな永く存するものにあらずして、一二十年ごとに必ず脩繕改造を待つ。いはんや、これを外にしては、応接給資の用あり、飼糧購賞の費あるをや。おほよそかくのごときの類は、まさに安くにかその給を取らんとするや。それ劣済困窮の家、多く賓客を得、しばしば宴饗を設けば、すなはちその資財空乏して、卒にまた継ぐべからざるに至ること、必せり。今の時事、何をもってかこれを経理するゆゑんのものは、何の術ぞ。経世に志あるものは、よろしく先づ審かに計るべきところなり。

as people who enjoy talking about politics and push their work aside. Study which has no use, and whose absence would cause nobody distress, is useless study. Useful study is, for example, like having light clothes for summer wear and fur coats for winter; people could not live if nobody made them.

In an Emperor's politics, standards for judging riches are placed at the side of the people. If the people have excess on their side, it is transferred to the state coffers; if they have shortage on their side, conversely, it is supplemented from the state coffers. This makes it impossible for the Emperor alone to be satisfied while farm labourers go hungry, or conversely, for farm labourers alone to be satisfied while the state goes hungry. The saying that "If a farmer were rich, how could the king still be poor? If a farmer were poor, how could the king still be rich?" is true in all epochs, both ancient and modern. Japan is said to be a rich country abounding in gold, silver, goods, rice and grain. On the other hand, since the size of the land is limited, the state does not have enough to spare after goods produced domestically are allotted to internal consumption. However, the need for naval defence was caused by external factors; the huge expenditure needed to build several hundred batteries, construct several hundred battleships and cast several thousand cannons has not been planned in the relationship between domestic product and domestic consumption up to now. In addition, these naval defence facilities are not properties that can be used forever once produced, but must be repaired or modified without fail after ten or twenty years. Furthermore, there are the costs of holding exchange receptions with foreign countries and their diplomatic delegations, externally, while funds are also needed to maintain a military force for naval defence, internally. Just how can we raise the capital for this purpose? If a poor family often has to treat guests hospitably, it will eventually use up its fortune and suffer the misfortune of insolvency. I consider the present Japanese

予が*磽卦の著は、ただに武学の生徒に益あるのみならず、兼ねて国家の武備に裨あり。

往日、官その*鐫版を阻むは、吾その何の意たるかを知らず。

*先公は*相台に登り、嗣ぎて防海のことを管せり。時に英夷は清国に寇し、*声勢相逮べり。予、時事に感慨し、上書して策を陳べたり。実に*天保壬寅十一月なりき。後に清の*魏源の聖武記を観るに、また時事に感慨するによりて著はすところにして、その書の序は、またこの歳の七月に作られたれば、すなはち予の上書に先だつこと僅かに四月のみにして、しかもその論ずるところも、往々約せずして同じきものあり。ああ、予と魏とは、おのおの異域に生れ、姓名を相識らざるに、時に感じて言を著すもの、一に何ぞ奇なるや。真に海外の同志といふべし。ただ魏は、上世より以来、中国に海防ありて海戦なしといひ、遂に壁を堅くし野を清くして、*岸奸を*杜絶するをもって、防海の家法となせり。予はすなはち盛んに磽・艦の術を講じて、*邀撃の計をなし、駆逐防截してもつて賊の死命を外海に制せんと欲す。これを異なれりとなすのみ。

磽卦　易理によって西洋砲術を基礎づけようとした著作。嘉永五年（一八五二）に書かれたが、幕府の許可がおりず、公刊できなかった。

鐫版　印刷出版。

先公　松代藩主真田幸貫。松平定信の子、真田家の養子となり、文政六年（一八二三）八月に家督を嗣ぎ、嘉永五年五月に隠居し、翌六月に死去した。

相台　老中の地位。幸貫は天保一二年（一八四一）六月より弘化元年（一八四四）五月まで老中であった。この間、天保一三年夏より一時海防係を担当している。

英夷は清国に寇し　アヘン戦争をさす。

声勢…　その情報と軍事的圧力が日本に及んできた。

天保壬寅　天保一三年（一八四二）。

魏源　清代の儒者、経世実用の学を志した。編著に『皇朝経世文編』がある。『聖武記』は清朝の初から道光年間にいたるまでの天子の武功を記すとともに、兵制などにもふれている。

闇合　期せずして符合する。

野を清くす　敵に利用されないために、家屋や田畑の穀物を除去する。

岸奸　上陸する敵。

杜絶　たつ。

邀撃　むかえうつこと。

防截　敵をふせぎたつ。

situation to be the same as this. In that case, how can we overcome such a crisis? Anyone who wants to take charge of politics must first have a plan regarding this.

I wrote *Hōka* not only for military pupils, but also with the aim of helping to establish a national defence system. But the Tokugawa Shogunate prohibited its publication. I cannot really understand why. When Yukitsura Sanada, the previous feudal lord of my Matsushiro Domain, attended as a member of the Shogun's Council of Elders, and was in charge of the military defence bureau, the United Kingdom invaded Qing China. And the extent of British power and force was thereby conveyed to Japan.
As I am sensitive to the situation, I advised the plan referred to above. This was in December 1842. After that, I looked at *Shengwu Ji* written by the Qing scholar Wei Yuan (1794-1857), and this also referred to the situation. The preface is dated August of the same year. In short, there is only a difference of four months compared to my letter of advice.

On top of that, the point of his argument is almost the same as mine, though there has been no meeting between us. Wei Yuan and I were born in different countries and did not even know each other's names. In spite of that, we decided to write suggestions and advice about the situation in the same year, and there is a strange consistency in the content of our opinions. What a very strange thing this is! This is indeed what I call a kindred spirit overseas. According to Wei Yuan's doctrine, however, China's traditional method of defence has involved preventing an approaching enemy from landing on the seashore. For this, they have made land preparations and reinforced their castle walls, because China has had no sea battles but only naval defence in the past. In contrast, my argument is that we should fight it out with sea battles, for which we should build warships and intercept the enemy at sea with artillery. This is the only point of difference between Wei Yuan and myself.

夷俗を馭するは、先づ夷情を知るに如くはなく、夷情を知るは、先づ夷語に通ずるに如くはなし。ゆゑに夷語に通ずるは、ただに彼を知るの楷梯たるのみならずして、またこれ彼を馭するの先務なり。予、窃かに深く念へらく、頃年諸藩、事に託して、しばしば舶を相房の間に寄するは、その情固より測り難しとなすと。因りて、皇国同文鑑若干巻を纂輯し、もつて欧羅諸国の語を通ずるの志あり。しかうして荷蘭は久しく互市の国たりて、邦人もまた多くその国の書を読むことを知れり。ゆゑに先づ荷蘭の部を刊せんと欲す。これより先、官より命ありて、おほよそ書籍を刊行するは、必ず官の看詳を経しむ。すなはち嘉永己酉の冬に、江都に来り、稿本を呈しもつて請へるも、遷延年を弥りて、卒に允さるるを得ざりき。その江都にあるの日に、始めて魏氏の書を獲てこれを読みしに、また内地に学を設け、専ら夷書・夷史を訳し、敵情を瞭悉し、もつて駕馭に補せんと欲せり。これまたその見の予と相符するものなり。ただ彼の国、今日能くその言を用ふるや否やを識らざるのみ。

互市　貿易通商。

官の看詳　幕府は弘化二年（一八四五）七月に、蘭書の翻訳出版はすべて天文方の許可を受けるよう通達した（それ以前は町奉行が検閲を担当していた）。

嘉永己酉　嘉永二年（一八四九）。

稿本　象山が『ヅーフ・ハルマ』を改訂して出版しようとした『増訂荷蘭語彙』の草稿。

瞭悉　明かに知りつくす。

駕馭　夷狄を統御すること。

符す　符合する。

夷俗　夷狄の風俗。

駆す　使ひこなす。

楷梯　はしご、手引。

託す　かこつける。

相房　相模と安房。

皇国同文鑑　外国語辞書のこと。

夷情　西洋諸国の科学技術などをさすものと考えられる。

To deal with the outlanders successfully, we must first of all know the actual situation of their country. And to know that actual situation, we have to be conversant with their language. In other words, becoming conversant with the outlanders' language is a way of knowing their country's actual situation and a major premise for dealing with them successfully.

In this respect, we failed to properly recognize the real intention when foreign ships approached the coast of the Kanto area with some specious pretence in the 1830s and 40s. Just as I had previously worried in private, it was because we were not conversant with the outlanders' language and therefore did not know the actual situation of their countries. Then I devised a plan to study and become conversant in European languages after editing some publications named *Kōkoku Dōbunkan*. I planned first to publish the section on the Dutch language, in particular, since trade between the Netherlands and Japan has continued for a long time and there are so many Japanese who can read Dutch books.

Before that, an order had been issued to the effect that the Shogunate's censorship was required when publishing books, so I requested permission after submitting the manuscript to Edo in the winter of 1849. But I received no reply before the old year ended, and eventually permission was refused.

While I was staying in Edo awaiting a reply from the Shogunate, I obtained the publication by Wei Yuan that I mentioned earlier. This publication also insisted that it would contribute to negotiating with foreign countries if their situations could be clarified by establishing schools for the translation of their books and histories. This is completely the same as my opinion. However, I don't know whether China has adopted Wei Yuan's theory or not.

海防の要は礁と艦とにありて、礁は最も首に居れり。魏氏の海国図識の中に、銃礁の説を輯めたるは、類ねみな粗漏無稽にして、児童の戯嬉の為のごとし。おほよそ事は自からこれをなさずして、能くその要領を得るものはこれなし。魏の才識をもってしても、しかもこれをこれ察せざりき。今の世に当りて、身に礁学なく、この謬妄を貽し、反って後生を誤りしは、吾、魏のために深くこれを惜しむ。

去夏、墨虜は兵艦四隻をもって、その国書を護送し、浦賀の澳に抵れり。その挙動詞気は、ことに悖慢を極め、国体を辱しむること細ならず、聞くもの切歯せざるはなかりき。時に某人は浦賀を鎮せしが、気を屏して負屈し、遂に能くなすことなく、虜の退きて後に、自から小刀を抽きて、その遺るところの虜主の画像を寸断し、もって怒を洩しぬ。昔、宋の曹瑋は、謫せられて陝西に官せしが、趙元昊の人となりを聞きて、すなはち画を善くするものをしてその貌を図せしめ、これをその英物にして必ず辺患をなさんことを知るものをしてその貌を図せしめ、これをその英物にして必ず辺患をなさんことを知り、預じめ辺備を講ぜんと欲して、人才を蒐閲せしに、後果してその言のごとくなりき。

しからばすなはち、その肖影を観るも、またもつてその能否を見て、吾が予備に資すべし。某人の知慮ここに及ばずして、毀ちてこれを滅したるは、惜しむべきのみ。ああ、均しく夷人なり、均しく画像なるに、或いは無くしてこれを求め、或いは有りてこれを毀つ。その知の深浅、謀の長短は、一に何ぞ遠きや。

海国図識　『海国図志』が正しい。アヘン戦争後に林則徐が翻訳せしめた西洋人の著作をもとにして、魏源が著した世界地理書で、一八四二年の六十巻本と一八五二年の百巻本がある。日本には前者が一八五四年ないし五三年に輸入され、横井小楠、橋本左内らも耽読した。その一部は訓点をつけて翻刻、もしくは和訳出版され、ペリー来航直後に日本人の世界知識を拡げる上で、重要な役割を演じた。

無稽　でたらめ。
戯嬉　たわむれ。
謬妄　あやまり。
悖慢　ことばづかい、辞気、道理にもとりたかぶること。
墨虜　アメリカという夷狄。
去夏　嘉永六年(一八五三)六月三日に来航した。
国体　国家の体面。
某人　戸田氏栄。弘化四年(一八四七)より浦賀奉行であった。
気を屏す　息を止める、恐れるさまをいう。
負屈　屈伏。
曹瑋　宋の将軍。
趙元昊　西夏の景帝。々夏州に拠り西に叛き夏を建国し、しばしば宋軍を敗った。のちに宋と和し西夏王に冊せられる。元昊の祖は代々夏州に拠り西平王に封ぜられていた。元昊は宋に叛き夏を建国し、しばしば宋軍を敗った。のちに宋と和し西夏王に冊せられる。
辺患　外敵が国境をおかすうれい。
蒐閲　あつめみる。
予備　あらかじめそなえること。

The key points of naval defence are artillery and warships; guns, in particular, are most important. Although *Hai Guo Tu Zhi* (Illustrated Treatise on the Maritime Kingdoms) by Wei Yuan refers to guns, the content is crude and childish. In everything, it is rather difficult to grasp the key points without actual experience. But even a talented person such as Wei Yuan did not realize this. He wrote down his theories with mistakes like this, due to insufficient knowledge of gun tactics, thus causing confusion for generations to come. I deeply regret this on his behalf. Last summer, Americans with state documents and four warships visited the port of Uraga. Their behaviour and way of talking were extremely overbearing, and inflicted a severe wound on the pride of Japan as a nation. Everyone who heard them gnashed their teeth in vexation. At that time, one Uraga magistrate succumbed to his frustration, and in the end didn't receive the visitors properly. After the Americans had withdrawn, leaving behind a portrait of the American President as a gift, he let out all his frustration by taking a knife and cutting the picture into pieces. In the old days of the Song era, while Cao Wei was a government employee after he had been delegated to Shaanxi, he heard of Zhao Yuanhao and had a good painter make a picture of Zhao's face. When he saw the picture, he decided that this outstanding person would definitely cause a disturbance. He therefore fortified the national borders and made efforts to gather talented persons around him for purposes of defence. But in the end, it happened just as he had feared. As this shows, a portrait provides material evidence for judging a person's character and preparing for the future. The magistrate of Uraga could not think that far, and destroyed such an important portrait. It really is a matter for regret. The opponents were foreigners in both cases, and the object was also a portrait. However, one side took the trouble to make a painting, while the other side destroyed a precious picture that had been received as a gift. What a fine state of affairs! How clearly are the intelligent

今春　安政元年(一八五四)一月一六日に来航。
便坐　休息所。
約束　とりしまり、命令。
公　藩主をさす。
不虞　害、よくないこと。
牛角天䃟　臼砲(モルチール)の一種。
望月貫恕　通称は主水、松代藩の定府家老。→
軍議に参ぜり　象山は嘉永六年一一月より海防のための軍議役に任命されていた。
短兵　みじかい兵器、刀剣の類。
咫尺　近い距離、咫は八寸。
利兵　鋭利な武器。
一薙　ひとなぎ。
斫断　たちきる。
長巻　太刀を長く作り、それに長い柄をつけて紐などを巻いたもの。人馬の足などをなぎ倒すのに用いる。

　今春、墨虜の来たるや、□官は便坐を横浜に設け、もって応接の所となし、松城・小倉の二藩に命じ、兵を発してもってこれを護衛せしめ、かつ約束を接待の官吏に聴かしめたり。初め吾が□公の命を受くるや、真に虜の不虞に備ふと以為へり。すなはち野戦䃟二門、牛角天䃟三門、銃卒百名、刀槍士五十名を発し、国老望月貫恕をもってこれを督せしめ、予はその軍議に参ぜり。謂へらく、接待の官吏、兵を知らず、吾と小倉とをもって一横一直に対して陣せしめん。銃手はもって威を逞しくすべし。もしそれ兵を知らずして、相接すること咫尺にして、変倉卒に起らば、彼、銃技に精しといへども、我、利兵をもってこれに乗じ、一薙して数頭を斫断すべしと。すなはち別に長巻二十把を備へ、もって従はしむ。

divided from the unintelligent, the prudent from the rash.

This spring, when the Americans came back to Japan, the Shogunate provided a rest area for them in Yokohama, indicating this to be used as a reception space, and commanded the Matsushiro and Okura Domains to guard it with common soldiers. The method of guarding the space was to be agreed between the foreigners and the government official in the reception group.

First of all, when the Head of the Matsushiro Domain received the Shogunate's command, the impression was that we were being mobilized to prepare against illegal acts by the Americans. Accordingly, the chief retainer Kannyo Mochizuki started off at the head of a party with two field guns, three mortars, 100 soldiers with firearms and 50 soldiers with Japanese swords and spears.

I accompanied this party as a staff officer, and had the following thoughts at that time. If the government official in the reception group had known military strategy, he would have given full play to the effect of guns, for example, by making the Matsushiro group encamp horizontally and the Kokura group vertically. If he didn't know military strategy, he would have made them encamp opposite each other with the Americans in between. In that case, we would have had no choice but to fight with swords, because we could not have used the guns.
If we had encamped near the American party and an incident were to occur, our skilled samurai would have had no problem in putting the enemy to the sword, however skilful the Americans were at handling guns. So I had twenty swords provided separately.

吾が兵の*金川に至るや、官吏は人をして謂はしめて曰く、「大磯は必ず前駅に賽き、横浜の地に引き入るることなかれ」と。望月は対へて曰く、「吾が藩は命を奉じて応接の場を護衛す。大磯は変に備ふるゆゑんなり。これを隔地に賽かば、変、*非時に発せば、もつて卒かなるに応じ難し。敢へて辞す」と。官吏曰く、「今玆の応接は、万々その変なきを保すべし。不幸にしてまさに変あらんとすれば、即時に*官丁を発し、磁器を搬運し、決して貴藩をして欠乏あらしめず。今大磯をもつて横浜に入らば、夷人は或いはその守衛の厳なるを憚りて、他地に移るを請はん。官の*累なり」と。望月はやむを得ずしてこれに従ひ、護衛の地を相るに及びて、「□官の命じて約束を聴かしむるものは、ほとんどこれなるか」と。官吏曰く、「東は*海涘に起り、西行すること二百歩にして、折れて北行することまたかくのごとし。これその所なり」と。予これを聞きて*驚駭す。

金川　神奈川。
非時　突然。
官丁　幕府の人夫。
海涘　海のほとり。
歩　六尺。
驚駭　おどろく。

But when our domain's military party had advanced as far as Kanagawa, the government official in the reception party sent a messenger to say that the cannon should be kept one post station back, and should not be taken to Yokohama. Mochizuki responded that he could not accept such an instruction, protesting that our domain's mission was to guard the reception area under orders from the Shogunate, and that the cannon was to be used if an incident occurred. If the cannon were left so far away, we would be unable to cope with the enemy should an incident occur.

Then the government official argued further that, first of all, we were to make sure such an incident could absolutely not happen in this reception. If the worst should come to pass, the Shogunate would immediately send men to have the cannon transported, and accordingly our domain would not have to be troubled. If the cannon were taken there now, the American party might feel surprised at the unduly zealous nature of our guard, and might then want to change the reception area, causing inconvenience to the Shogunate.

 Mochizuki was thus compelled to obey. But he was very dissatisfied with the Shogunate's order to the government official in the reception party, and wondered if this was the right way to reach an agreement with the foreigners.

When we eventually arrived at the area to be guarded, the government official asked us to guard a baseline that could be reached by taking 200 paces west from the east coast, followed by 200 paces north from there. I was astonished to hear this.

区処　手配。

集会　よりあつまること。

壊隳　やぶりくずされる。

　その地を詳にするに、南は応接の便坐を距ること二百歩を下らずして、民屋樹林のその間にあるあり。初め江戸にありしとき、竊かに意へらく、官吏は兵を諳んぜずといへども、自から国体あり、かつ二藩の兵を得ば、まさに密に便坐を囲繞し、もつて警禦を厳にすべしと。図らざりき、その区処の陋なること、ここに至らんとは。因りて建議して曰く、「大磯はすなはち官吏これを停めたれば、今あるところのものは小銃のみ。小銃の、力を逞しくするは、百歩のうちにあらずんば不可なり。かつ銃卒は百名を踰えず、短兵を執るものは五十名に過ぎず。夷虜が集会のところを距たること、遠く二百歩の外に陣し、また散じて三、四百歩の間田に守らば、ただ警察に益なきのみならずして、まさにもつて虜の侮慢を導くに足らん。去歳浦賀の応接は、護衛に法なくして、夷虜これを嗤ひ、邦人これを恥づ。しかも少しも省悟せずして、今またこの児戯をなす。官吏の不肖は固より道ふに足らず。本藩の武功盛名も、この輩に壊隳せらるるは、あに忍ぶべけんや」と。

On checking the details of the designated area, the southern area was more than 200 paces from the American rest area to the north, and furthermore, there were private houses and trees in between. What I had anticipated while still at Edo was that, however little the government official knew about military strategy, he would of course understand the structure of the land.

And I thought he would lay out a very severe state of alert in which we would secretly surround the American rest area, because we could use the soldiers of both the Matsushiro and Kokura Domains freely. I would never have imagined that we would be allocated so wrongly.

So then, I made the following proposal:

"Our party has only small guns now, since the government official has prohibited us from bringing in the cannon. To give full play to a gun's power, it must be fired within 100 paces. Besides, we have only 100 gunmen and 50 swordsmen. If we set our battle camp at a distance of 200 paces or more from the American rest area, then disperse and make a formation to defend the farmland 300 to 400 paces away separately, we will not only be of no use as a guard but will also win the contempt of the barbarians. When we received them at Uraga Bay last year, we incurred the ridicule of the barbarians due to the unreadiness of our guard, and felt shame because of it. And in spite of that bitter experience, again we act like children at play. Even if the ignorance of public servants can no longer be helped, I cannot endure this injury to our reputation for military exploits in the Matsushiro Domain."

すなはち望月と謀り、人をして備ふるにあらずして、夷虜のために邦民を禁呵するは、固より士大夫を煩はすべからず、また兵器に用なし。巡路ごとに、健児一、二名を出だして、青竹の杖を執りてこれを誰何せしめば、足らん。ただ江戸にて受くるところの命は、すなはちもつて廃すべからざれば、応接の日に、吾が藩はまさに別に士卒を出だして、陣を山間に整へ、もつて非時の変に備ふべきのみ。これ、公等の事を敗らず、また吾が職を墜さず、あにまた両得ならずや」と。官吏復して曰く、「言みな理に当る。しかれども、□官が両藩の人士を発するのことは、吾が輩すでにこれを夷人に告げたり。もしその人を出だざずして、陣を隠僻の地に設けば、夷人は必ず吾に異志あるを疑ひ、応接諧はざらん。これまた□官の累なり。必ず曲げて吾が言に従へ。その布陣の収散離合のごときのままなれば、吾が輩敢へて掣肘せず」と。予と望月とは、憤慨して楽しまずといへども、ただ意の命ずるのみに従ふ。当日に一哨を作り、これを田畝の間に置き、もつてその責を塞げり。ああ、国用を耗損し、士卒を勤労せしめ、思慮計画を尽して、児戯をなすに同じきは、浩歎に付すべきなるのみ。

巡路　こみち。

禁呵　しかりとりしまる。

これ　幕府の官吏。

隠僻の地　へんぴでかくれた場所。

異志　ふたごころ。

憤慨　いきどほる。

一哨　一つのみはり。

耗損　へらす。

浩歎　大いになげくこと。

After consulting with Mochizuki, I then sent a messenger to the government official with the following statement based on the above opinion: "If we encamp in line with your policy, we will only regulate the actions of Japanese people toward the barbarians; we will not be guarding to prevent the barbarians from committing acts of violence. We would not have needed to dispatch recognized clansmen and provide weapons if our only plan had been to control Japanese people's behaviour. It would have sufficed to position one or two burly men with bamboo sticks to check those passing on each route. On the other hand, because we must obey the orders from Edo, we are going to prepare for the worst case by pitching camp on the mountain side with another party from our domain on the day of the reception. If we do that, your policy will be maintained, and we will also execute our duty. It will be like killing two birds with one stone." However, the government official replied: "I quite agree with your opinion, but I have already explained to them that the Shogunate will set up a guard by commanding the Matsushiro and Kokura Domains to the Americans' rest area. Therefore, if the party does not attend but pitches camp toward the mountains, the American side will suspect the Japanese side's intention, and the reception will not go well. And in that case, the Shogunate would be troubled. So I hope you will obey my policy and contain your anger. Instead, I will leave the methods of positioning and moving soldiers to your decision, without any interference from our side."

Although Mochizuki and I had no way of giving vent to our pent-up anger, there was nothing we could do.
On the day of the reception, we more or less fulfilled our responsibility by just setting a guard in the countryside. Although we went to great expense and made great efforts to make the soldiers work hard through planning by the leader and staff officer, the result was like chaperoning children at play. It was such a deplorable situation.

下田の議　下田開港の議。

倣ふ　土地・家などをかりる。

巣穴　すみか。

格塞　ふさがる。

形勝　地の利。

胆を嘗め薪に坐す　臥薪嘗胆、辛苦艱難して自から励ますことをいふ。

二月廿日の夜、*下田の議のほぼ定まるを聞く。翌朝早起して望月に詣りて曰く、「下田は本邦の要地にして、その形勢は全世界の喜望峰に比すべし。夷虜これを倣ひ、屯駐してもつて巣穴となさば、その害は言ふべからざらんなり。米穀布帛はみな海運に資る。不幸にして警ありて、海路*格塞せば、江戸はその南端にあり。その禍を受けん。伊豆の州たるや、天城の険、その中を隔絶して、下田はその南端にあり。一旦変起らば、陸路兵を出だすも、礟隊は嶮の沮むところとなりて、もつて行くべからず。海路はすなはち我に堅艦なし。他日たとひ造作するを得とも、虜に海陸の*形勝ありて、我は反つてこれを喪へば、主客位を易へ、攻守勢を殊にせん。計にあらざるなり。それ善く事を制するものは、常にその利をして我にありて、その害をして彼にあらしむ。今、已むを得ずして敵人に地を仮さんには、よろしく他日の計をなして、得るの処を択ぶべし。竊かに横浜の地勢を覧るに、甚だこれに称へり。海陸もて兵を進むるを得て常にここにあらしめば、江戸を去ること甚だ邇ければ、すなはち人々の胆を嘗め薪に坐するの念は、自から已む能はず。

As I heard that talks on opening Shimoda Port had more or less been decided on the night of February 20th, I got up early the next day and went to meet with Kannyo Mochizuki. Shimoda Port is a key place in Japan, its position being almost comparable with the Cape of Good Hope in global terms. If the foreigners were to lease land there, set up their base and then make it their hotbed, the damage to Japan would be considerable.

On the other hand, there is the Shogun's castle at Edo, which also has a large population. There, the necessities of life such as rice, grains and cloth all depend on marine transportation. If some unfortunate incident were to happen and the marine route were to close, Edo would be the first to suffer damage.

If an incident were to occur and Japanese troops were dispatched by travel overland, gun soldiers would not be able to advance, as the way is obstructed by steep mountains. If we wanted to use the sea route, on the other hand, Japan doesn't have warships that could withstand actual fighting. Even if Japan had plans to build warships in the near future, the enemy would already have obtained the advantage of the terrain, not only over land but also at sea, and so Japan would lose both. Host would change places with guest, and the relationship between offence and defence would be reversed.

Could such a stupid thing come to pass? A sharp-minded person would do something about it immediately, always keeping advantageous conditions on his own side and making sure potentially damaging conditions would go to the opponent's side.

Even if we cannot avoid leasing land to the enemy now, we must think well on the future and select a place that can be easily accessed by our forces, by both land and sea.

In this regard, Yokohama is actually a convenient location in terms of its terrain.

繋縻　つなぎしばる。

間は髪をもつてすることる能はず　間髪をいれない、さしせまっていること。

小林虎　小林虎三郎。

主侯　長岡藩主牧野忠雅、当時老中であった。

阿部閣老　阿部正弘、当時老中の筆頭であった。

親幸　したしみ可愛がっている人に会って。

規諫　ただしいさめる。

警衛守禦の方も、また自から厳ならざるを得ず。また親しく彼の長ずるところを観れば、もつて速かに我の智巧を進むべし。これ、その利多しとなすゆゑんなり。もし下田に退かば、すなはち人心は必ず弛み、守衛は必ず懈らん。しかも、虜の舶は迅速にして、もつて繋縻し難ければ、横浜にあると下田にあると、その江戸の腹心の患をなすこと、すなはち間は髪をもつてすること能はず。ゆゑに吾謂へらく、横浜をもつてこれに仮すの愈れりとなすに如かざるなりと。これ天下の大計なり。君、士卒を総べてここにあり、もつて黙すべからず。上書して□公に献策あらんことを乞ひて可なり」と。望月曰く、「然り。しかれども吾が上書するは、子の上言するに如かず」と。すなはち予に命じて、江戸に還り、これを□公に告げしむ。沮むものありて果さず。□公は予に許して、自からこれをなさしむ。ここにおいて竊かに建白するところあり。また、長岡の小林虎をして、その主侯に上書して、大計を開陳せしめ、また、これをして阿部閣老の親幸するところあらんに見えて、為にその利害を論ぜしめ、時に因りて規諫することを得て、挽回するところを欲す。並びにみな行はれず。小林生はこれをもつて主侯の譴を獲、遂に辞して国に帰れり。

If a foreign ship were to drop anchor there, all Japanese would maintain a mental state of alertness and naturally redouble their precautions, due to its proximity to Edo. They would also observe the foreigners' advantages directly, and this could speed up progress in knowledge and technology. Therefore, if Yokohama were made an open port, the benefit would be large. But if a far-off port like Shimoda were selected, the public feeling would first slacken and tend to neglect precaution. Furthermore, the foreigners' ships are very fast and we cannot keep them moored on the shore. As such, there would be almost no difference between Yokohama and Shimoda in terms of the danger of an enemy attack on Edo if something were to happen.   Considering these things in total, I think it would be best to lease Yokohama to the foreigners. This indeed is the grand state plan. You would not be able to keep your silence either, if you had come here at the head of some soldiers as I have done. Thus, I urged Mochizuki to write a letter to the feudal lord and have him make a proposal to the Shogunate. Mochizuki replied, "Your opinion is correct, but it would be much better if you said it directly to our feudal lord than if I were to write to him," and sent me back to Edo. Then I expressed my opinion to my feudal lord, but someone opposed the idea, and I could not get him to make my proposal to the Shogunate. The lord permitted me, however, to take independent action to put my idea into practice. So I secretly drew up a petition to the Shogunate, and meanwhile asked my subordinate Torasaburo Kobayashi (a Nagaoka clansman) to submit the letter about our grand plan to his lord. I asked him to wait for an opportunity when Abe (a member of the Shogunate's Council of Elders) approached him, then to explain the advantages and disadvantages to him, and if possible to petition him. I thus planned to reverse the decision to offer Shimoda as an open port. But the result was failure in both cases. Kobayashi received an official reprimand from his lord, eventually resigned from his post and returned to his home province.

曩に予、一、二の友生とともに、鎌倉の遊をなし、遂に海に泛びて荒岬を過ぎ、城島に抵り、三崎に泊し、松輪を歴て、宮田に宿し、浦賀に次し、猿嶼に上り、金沢に観、本牧に出でて都に還る。その往来の由るところ、防堵を設けて海寇に備ふるを観ること、無慮十余所、しかうして錯置みな法を得ずして、一の防蔽の選に当るべきものもなし。ここに至りて、覚えず天を仰ぎて浩歎し、胸を擗ちて流涕すること、これを久しうす。それ江都は天下の咽喉なり、富津の洲觜は、称して天険といへども、海口なほ闊し。戦艦水軍あるにあらずんば、固よりもつて敵人の侵擾窺伺を遏めがたし。今これをこれ務めずして、痴堵呆堞を設為し、高くこれを海表に掲ぐるは、これ我が謀なきを海外に示すなり。頃年、東西諸藩は、舶を寄せて遊偵すれば、あに我を軽んずるの心を開かざらんや。吏員は庸流なれば、固より讁むるに足らず。その金鞍華韉、綾衣肉食して、自から高く等類よりも出づといふものも、天下の大計を知らず、国の財用を糜し、もつてこの無益の務をなせんとする。因りて、上疏して海防の利病を論ぜんと欲し、もつて時政の万一を裨けんことを翼ふ。草を具して、これを□先公に請ふも、□先公許さざれば、遂に止めにき。これ墨夷のこと、初夏なり。後四年にして、果して墨夷のこと起れり。登時、□先公が予の上書を尼めしは、蓋し触忤して罪に抵るを懼れたればなり。その蓋覆の仁も、また大なり。今日、□先公をして世にありて、予が拘囚さるるを知らしめば、すなはちその憂労をなすは、またまさに何如なるべき。

囊に 嘉永三年(一八五〇)四月のことである。
錯置 措置。
胸を擗ちて 胸をうつ。わが国で、「胸をかきむしる」というのと同じ。
富津の洲觜 浦賀水道につきでている房総半島の部分。洲觜はなぎさの先端。
侵擾
窺伺 うかがいはかること。
痴堵呆堞 役にたたぬ堵堞。堞はもののみべい。
海表 海上。
庸流 凡庸な部類に属するもの。
金鞍華韉 はなやかなくらやくらの下おおい。
綾衣肉食 立派な衣服をき、美食すること。
等類 仲間・同朋。
馳突 突撃してくる。
折衝禦侮 敵のつきくるほこさきをくじき、そのあなどりをふせぐ。
上疏 上書する。疏は箇条書にしてのべること。
草 この草稿は全集第二巻に収録されている。
嘉永庚戌 嘉永三年(一八五〇)。
首夏 夏のはじめ、初夏をいう。
墨夷のこと ペリー来航をいう。登時 正しくは、即座の意であるが、そのとき、当時、の意に誤用したのであろう。
触忤 政法にふれさからう。
蓋覆の仁 仁の心で人をおおいつくしむこと。

Once, I took a trip to Kamakura with a few friends. On the way back, we took the sea route and stayed overnight at Misaki in Jogashima after passing Arasaki. Next we stayed at Miyata by way of Matsuwa, then passed through Uraga and returned to Edo by way of Honmoku after sightseeing at Kanazawa, where we climbed Mount Saruyama.

On the way, we made field trips to inspect about a dozen naval defence facilities in readiness for the barbarian invasion.

However, none of these facilities were fit for purpose, and not one of them was useful for defence. When I saw them, I looked up at the sky, beat my breast and cried out in vexation despite myself, as my tears flowed endlessly.

Edo is the throat of the whole country. Cape Futtsu is called a natural stronghold, but its sea gateway is still wide; it would be impossible to stop an enemy invasion without warships. However, the Shogunate makes not the slightest effort to this end; all it has done is to build useless, stupid cannon batteries and embankments, thus raising and exposing the coast. This is like announcing to foreign countries that the Japanese government will do nothing. American and European ships have been approaching and scouting there since quite recently, and when they see it, they probably look down on Japan. What can we do with idiots like those Shogunate officials?

What I absolutely cannot forgive, however, is that our feudal lords always wear gaudy armour, eat richly and dress luxuriously, yet they have no knowledge of state politics, but spend the national budget on building useless facilities. I have no idea how they intend to protect or defend against a barbarian warship attack if it really came to pass.

When I thought this, I planned to write to the Shogunate with a discussion of the present state and measures for naval defence, hoping that this could contribute in some way to the national defence. I drew up a rough draft and asked for the previous lord's approval. But the previous lord did not approve this, and so the

川路司農　幕末の勘定奉行、川路左衛門尉聖謨。嘉永五年(一八五二)五月に大坂町奉行より勘定奉行に栄転した。司農は勘定奉行をさすが、もともとは漢代に財政をつかさどった官名。

上書に擬せし旧稿　上書のつもりで書いた昔の草稿。

傾倒　のらずいう。

故常　しきたり、習慣。

急務十事　急務十事ないし急務十条として伝えられているのは、以下の十条である。

其一　堅固の船を備へ、水軍を練るべき事

其二　城東の砲台を新築し、相房の砲台を改築すべき事

其三　志気精鋭・筋骨強壮の者を選び、大砲隊を編成すべき事

其四　慶安度(慶安年間)の軍制を改正すべき事

其五　砲政を定め、広く硝田を開くべき事

其六　警急の為め、将材を選ぶべき事

其七　其短を舎て其長を用ひ、其名に循はず其実を講ずべき事

其八　綱紀を正し、士気を振ふべき事

其九　大小銃を演習し、四時、間断なからしむる事

其十　諸藩海防人数、聯事の法を以て編成すべき事

吉田生の獄　吉田松陰の密航失敗事件。

*川路司農は、大坂市尹より転任し、防海のことを与かり聞く。予、旧より厚交あれば、*上書に擬せし旧稿を出だしてこれに示し、近都の防堵が修築に法なくして、実用に適せざるを極言せしも、司農またいまだ甚だしくはこれを信ぜざりき。ここにおいて、始めて深く予が言を納る。一日予に謂ひて曰く、「子、言ふところあらんと欲せば、吾、能くこれを閣老に達せん」と。予曰く、「僕の言はんと欲するところは、君の為に傾倒してほとんど尽せり。君、能くこれを言ひ、君、能くこれを行はば、天下の福なり。僕はただ天下の福を求むるのみ。上書して名を釣るは、その本心にあらざるなり」と。人材を選びて、船を海外に購ふの策を論ずるに及びて、司農に沮む色あり。予曰く、「これ当今先務の急なり。しかるに、君なほ故常に牽掣せられて、発言する能はず。他になほ何をか望まん。僕まさに上書して、もってこれを道ふべし」と。すなはち急務十事を条疏し、司農に因りて、これを阿部閣老に上る。報あらず。*吉田生の獄起るに至りても、また少しも明察を蒙らず。故常の変じ易からず、時勢の明かにすべからざるは、かくのごとし。知らず、天下の大計は、まさに何れの日にしてか能く立たんとするや。

plan came to an end. This was at the beginning of summer 1850. And four years later, sure enough, the US fleet encroached on Edo Bay. At that time, the previous lord did not approve of my letter, because he would have felt sorry for me if I had been incriminated for going against the Shogunate's intention. I can only thank him for his benevolence. Today, if the previous lord were still alive and had seen me put in prison, how greatly he would have grieved over the situation.

After a while, Toshiakira Kawaji's position changed from Osaka town magistrate to the Commissioner of Finance. He also held the post of Naval Officer. As I had been good friends with him in former times, I showed him the draft letter that had ended without being submitted, and sternly criticized the method of using cannon batteries for Edo's defence as being unfit for purpose. Kawaji didn't trust me too much at that time. But when the US fleet encroached there, he came to ask my opinion for the first time, as everything had gone according to my prediction.

One day, Kawaji suggested that I contact a member of the government if I had some opinion to express. I answered that I had already informed him of my idea, and that I would leave the rest to him. He should convey my opinion and have it carried out. Then the world would be in order. I said I only wished that the world should be in order, and had no wish to make a name for myself by writing the letter.

Of my opinions, Kawaji was opposed to the scheme whereby the Shogunate would select and dispatch personnel to purchase ships overseas. So I emphasized that this was the most important assignment.

"If you stick to the old policy of isolation and do not propose it to the Shogunate in spite of that, there is nothing for it. Let me write the letter directly myself," I said. So I drafted the *Ten Urgent Articles*, then submitted them to Abe, a member of the government, through Kawaji. But it had no effect. The sanction

諳厄児　英国。

屏す　まもる。

　江戸の海口の防戦は、利、礮台にあり。その形勢の欠くるところは、全く別に礮艘を備へ、機を相て策応するにあり。しかれども、その力を得るのところは、海中にただ一、二区を置きて足れり。必ずしも多くこれを築かず。ゆゑに能くその要を得ば、陸続相連なれり。これ、荷蘭・諳厄児の策は、拠るべきなり。今なすところのごとき、海口にてもつて洋寇を待つの術にあらざるなり。蓋し陸戦は、攻中に守を寓し、守中に攻を寓す。その守るに方りてや、塁をもつて自から屏し、もつて自から屏するの法にして、塁中の人に係る。その塁を多くせざること能はず。その攻むるに方りてや、並びに塁中の人衆ければ、塁を出でてもつて衝く。その守ると攻むるとは、固よりその塁を多くなはち然らず。礮台の兵は礮艘を操らずして、きを貴ばずして、礮艘を操るなり。蓋し礮台多ければすなはち兵分れ、兵分るればすなはち士を用ふること衆くして、左のものは右を拯ふ能はず、右のものは左を救ふ能はず。不幸にして賊船、中間に出でば、左右の台は障礙を相為して、礮を用ふる能はず。

imposed when Shoin Yoshida planned to leave the country illegally was also the same as before. Nothing has changed.
Old laws are thus not easily overturned; the times are not easily understood. When exactly will a far-sighted policy for the whole country be established?

We need batteries at the entrance to Edo Bay. I have insisted on this many times in the past. Though batteries generally have the advantage in a defensive battle at the entrance to a bay, if the topography is not so good, the battle force has to be supplemented by installing more batteries. But to supplement the battle force, it would be most effective to prepare other batteries, then aim the cannon in the necessary direction after checking the battle situation. If only that could be achieved, we would not need so many; just one or two batteries would be enough. On this point, we should learn from the examples of the Netherlands and the United Kingdom.
However, there are currently too many batteries surrounding the entrance to Edo Bay. This is the tactic whereby an army entrenches itself by building bastions, but it is not a method of defence against invading enemy warships at the entrance to a bay.
In a battle on land, there are defensive strategies when attacking and attacking strategies when defending. Bastions are used for self-protection when defending, but when turning to attack, soldiers can leave the bastions to rush the enemy. The same soldiers are deployed for both defence and attack, and because, on the battlefield, there are so many cases when the whole party rushes out to attack and others when they all take guard, more bastions must be built if there are more soldiers. Moreover, building too many bastions causes no obstruction.
But a battle at the entrance to a bay is a different matter altogether. Battery soldiers are specialized in that role and do not travel on warships. And warship sailors do not work on batteries.

匱乏　とぼしい。
進剿　前進して撃滅する。
讋服　おそれ服させる。
某地の県令某氏　伊豆韮山の代官、江川太郎左衛門英竜をさす。
当道　当局者。

悪にぞあるその利たることや。かつ礟艘匱乏して、進剿するに術なくんば、もし賊、船を相房の間に連ねて、もって我が海運を絶たば、何をもってかこれを却けん。この時に当りて、たとひ内港に百の礟台ありとも、また無用に属す。戦はずして屈することなからんと欲すといへども、得べからざるなり。もしすなはち多く礟艘を備へ、訓練するに時をもつてし、開戦策応せば、可ならざるところなく、もって洋賊を讋服して、その死命を制するに足らん。また何を苦しんで、海中にこの許多の礟台をもってするをなさんや。多事の際、その経費もまた甚だ惜しむべし。某地の県令某氏は、小しく才幹あるも、素より学問なし。西洋陸戦の塁図を見て、その解を知らず、杜撰牽合して、もって海口を守るの策をなす。予深くその非を識りて、しばしばこれを川路司農に言ひしに、司農やや予が言を信然す。当道もまた深くこれを究めず、もって是となして施行せり。しかれども遂に救ふ能はざりき。これまた慨すべきなり。

As such, there is no need to install too many batteries, but it's fine to have a lot of warships. If there are too many batteries, the troops are separated; and if the troops are separated, more fighting personnel are needed.

Moreover, the battery on the left cannot rescue the one on the right, and the battery on the right cannot rescue the one on the left. If an enemy warship were to come through the centre, the batteries on the left and right would hold their fire for fear of hitting each other. The advantage held by the battery side would be eliminated.

Again, if we concentrate on batteries and have few warships, there will be no way of destroying the enemy warships by attacking them. If the enemy were to cut off our sea route by lining up warships side by side between Sagami and Awa, how could we disperse them? Even if we had several hundred batteries in the sea, they would be of no use. We could not even engage in battle, and would lose.

But if we were to provide a large number of warships and take time to train the personnel, we could adopt any plan should a war break out. In that case, we would overwhelm the foreigners, and the victory would be ours. Why do we need to expend energy in building so many batteries? In these days of crisis and upheaval, the expense would surely be too great. Some official in some prefectural office, a man with some talent but no learning, saw a drawing of bastions used in a western land war, then, in spite of having no understanding of the distinction between land war and sea war, made a proposal for batteries to protect the bay entrance by twisting the details to suit his own ends. The responsible government official then adopted this proposal without due consideration, and executed it just as it was.

I noticed this mistake from the beginning and repeatedly warned Toshiakira Kawaji, the Commissioner of Finance. But although he seemed to believe some of what I said, in the end he did nothing. It is a matter of such regret.

千羊の皮は、一狐の腋に如かず。しかうして千金の裘は、また一狐の皮にあらず。今、千金の裘を為らんと欲せば、これを屠羊の家に徴すべきなり。厚くしてこれを利し、導きて苟くもその心を得ば、五州の人、みな得て使ふべきなり。何ぞいはんや我が民をや。

これを舎かば、敵間の来りて我を間するものも、また我が用をなさん。

予、年二十以後は、すなはち匹夫も一国に繋ることあるを知る。三十以後は、すなはち天下に繋ることあるを知る。四十以後は、すなはち五世界に繋ることあるを知る。

おほよそ五十七条

千羊の皮は一狐の腋に如かず 『史記』趙世家。

千金の裘はまた一狐の皮にあらず 『説苑』建本。

五州 五大州。

舎かば おいておくならば。

敵間 敵の間諜。

一国 松代藩をさす。

天下 日本全体をさす。

五世界 五大州、つまり地球全体をいう。

A thousand sheepskins are not worth a single fox's armpit skin. And a priceless leather bag could not be made with that single fox's skin.

In Japan today, we should be making priceless leather bags, but we seek the materials in a slaughterhouse for sheep. They cannot be made that way.
If we could just grasp the spirit of that, we could use everybody in the world to our advantage. If we were to treat them politely and keep them handy under good leadership, even the enemy who had come for scouting could be won over to our side.

So is it possible that our nation's people cannot be used?

When I was 20,
I could act and think on the scale of a whole domain.
At 30, I knew how to act and think on the scale of Japan.
Today, at past 40, I must think on a global scale,
and act with appropriate magnanimity.

紺野博士編、佐久間象山『省諐録』英訳書の上梓を慶ぶ

笠谷和比古
帝塚山大学文学部教授
国際日本文化研究センター名誉教授
京都大学文学博士

　このたび佐久間象山の『省諐録』が紺野大介博士の英語翻訳をもって公刊される運びとなった。日本人として、またこの時代の歴史を研究する者として喜び一入である。
　紺野先生の専門は自然科学系ながら、日本の思想、殊に幕末の英傑たちの思想に御造詣が深く、それらすぐれた幕末人士の思想を現代の日本人にはもとより、広く海外の人にも知ってもらいたいという思いを抱かれるようになった。これまでに橋本左内の『啓発録』、吉田松陰の『留魂録』の二著を世に送り出されており、本書の佐久間象山『省諐録』はその第三作目にあたる。
　私と紺野先生との関係を申すならば、2009年2月に北京日本学研究センター・中華日本哲学会共同主催の形をもって、「武士道」を主題とする中国・韓国・日本の研究者による多国際シンポジウムが北京の外国語学院において開催されたが、その会議でお会いして以来のことになる。そのような御縁もあって、このたび先生の御労作完成への祝辞かたがた一文を草する次第である。
　佐久間象山と『省諐録』については紺野先生の本書解説に詳しいが、幕末史上における重要人物の著述物であるだけに、蛇足の誹りを顧みず一、二述べておきたい。
　獄中での思索を書き連ねた『省諐録』には、養生論、学問観、処世訓など様々な議論が見られて興味深いものがある。子孫への戒めと親心の細やかさなども垣間見られ、象山の人となりが偲ばれて微笑ましくもある。し

On the Publication of "Record of Conscience", Dr.Daisuke Konno's English Translation of *Seikenroku* by Sakuma Shozan

Kazuhiko Kasaya
Professor, Faculty of Letters, Tezukayama University
Emeritus Professor, International Research Center of Japanese Studies
Doctor of Literature, Kyoto University

As both a native of Japan and a historical scholar of the period in question, I am delighted to know that Sakuma Shozan's *Seikenroku* is now to be published in English translation as "Record of Conscience" by Dr Daisuke Konno.

Although Dr Konno's expertise lies in natural sciences, he is deeply knowledgeable about Japanese thought, and has a particularly keen interest in the great thinkers of Japan's Bakumatsu period. For this reason, he has made it his quest to convey the ideas of these prominent late-Edo personalities, not only to contemporary Japanese readers but also to others around the world. True to this quest, he has already published English translations of *Keihatsuroku* ("Treatise on Enlightenment") by Hashimoto Sanai and *Ryūkonroku* ("Soulful Minute") by Yoshida Shoin, making Sakuma Shozan's "Record of Conscience" his third publication of this kind.

I first met Dr Konno at a multinational symposium co-hosted by the Beijing Center for Japanese Studies and the Chinese Society for Studying Japanese Philosophies in February 2009. The symposium, held at Beijing University of Foreign Languages, was on the theme of "Bushido" (the Way of the Warrior) and was attended by researchers from China, South Korea and Japan. Thanks partly to this lucky coincidence, I now find myself writing these few words of congratulation on the completion of Dr Konno's labours.

While Dr Konno's own introduction to this book will provide detail on Sakuma Shozan and his "Record of Conscience", I hope I may be permitted to add one or two comments of my own, if only because this publication concerns an important figure in late Edo history.

"Record of Conscience", a collection of Sakuma Shozan's thoughts while in prison, offers very interesting insights into a number of topics, including curative medicine, academic learning and lessons in life. It also gives glimpses of warnings

かしやはり同書の真骨頂が、その経世論、国防論にあることは論を俟たないであろう。

そこには国家の危機の意識が濃厚であった。当時の世界の情勢は、欧米列強による世界制覇のただ中にあった。世界の各地は欧米列強の植民地へと編入されつつあり、世界五大州のうち四つまでが、すでにヨーロッパ人の支配するところとなっていた。そして残るアジアについても、インドやビルマ・マレーシア・シンガポールはイギリスの、インドネシアはオランダの、フィリピンはアメリカの植民地へとそれぞれ編入されていた。ヴェトナム・カンボジア・ラオスなどのインドシナもまた、象山の時代から少し遅れてフランスの植民地となる。

そして中国である。清朝中国は1840年代のアヘン戦争でイギリスの攻撃を受けて敗退し、香港の割譲を余儀なくされた。さらに1960年の第二次アヘン戦争(アロー号事件)においては首都北京が英仏連合軍によって占領され、結果、不平等条約の締結を余儀なくされ半植民地化の途を歩みつつあった。

『省譽録』はこのような世界情勢、アジアの危機の中で考察され、記されていることに留意する必要がある。彼が欧米列強に対して「夷狄(野蛮人)」という激しい非難の言辞を執拗に繰り返し用いているのはこの故である。日本はまさに国家存亡の危機のただ中にあった。その対応を誤るならば、中国のように半植民地の途をたどるか、さらにはインド・ヴェトナムのように完全に欧米列強の植民地に組み込まれるかであった。

このような危機の中で、日本はいかにして国家としての独立を保ちうるであろうか。そこでは徒に欧米列強を「夷狄(野蛮人)」と罵るだけではだめである。欧米列強が世界制覇をなしえた力の秘密、その源泉を究明する必要がある。彼はこのようにして洋学と欧米文明の世界へと分け入っていく。他の多くの学者、言論人たちが精神論による攘夷を叫ぶ中にあって、象山は冷静、客観的に西洋の学問を見つめていく。

本来的に儒学、朱子学の専門家をもって任じる象山にとって、西洋の学問が進んでいることを認めるというのは受け入れ難いことであったろうが、事実は事実として認め、更に積極的に西洋の学に取り組んでいく。そ

to his descendants and the depth of his parental feelings, among others, as charming reminders of Shozan's personality. It is surely beyond debate, however, that the true value of his book lies in Shozan's theories on state affairs and national defence.

In those theories, we find a rich awareness of a nation under impending crisis. The state of the world at the time was one of global domination by Western powers. These were extending their colonial territories to every corner of the globe, and four of the world's five continents had already been brought under European dominion. The only one left was Asia, but even there, Great Britain had colonies in India, Burma, Malaysia and Singapore, the Dutch had Indonesia, and the Americans had colonized the Philippines. Moreover, Vietnam, Cambodia, Laos and other parts of Indochina were to be colonized by the French some time after Shozan's day.

Then there was China. Under the Qing Dynasty, China was defeated by Britain in the First Opium War in the 1840s, when it was forced to cede Hong Kong. Again, at the end of the Second Opium War in 1860 (the Arrow incident), the capital Peking (Beijing) was occupied by Anglo-French forces, forcing the Chinese into an unequal treaty and taking them down the path toward semi-colonization.

It must be borne in mind that "Record of Conscience" was conceived and written against the backdrop of this world situation and crisis in Asia. This explains why Shozan persistently and repeatedly uses the rhetoric of harsh disapproval toward the Western powers, calling them "*iteki* (barbarians)". Indeed, Japan was in the very midst of a crisis of national survival. A mistaken response to this crisis might take Japan down the path to semi-colonization, as in China, or even to complete colonization by the Western powers, as in India and Vietnam.

Faced by this crisis, what should Japan do to maintain her independence as a sovereign state? It would not suffice merely to curse the Western powers as "barbarians". The secret or source of the power that had enabled them to dominate the world would need to be investigated. With this in mind, Shozan delved deep into the world of Western science and civilization. While many other scholars and commentators clamoured for the expulsion of foreigners based on spiritual arguments, Shozan examined Western learning with calm objectivity.

As an expert in Confucian and Neo-Confucian learning, it must have been hard for Shozan to accept that Western

して何事も徹底的に究めなければ止まない象山は、オランダ語を修得し、オランダ語原書を自由に読みこなし、西洋の最新情報を直接に獲得する術を手にする。

それを踏まえて欧米列強の力の源である、軍事技術の取得に努める。そしてここでも注目すべきことは、ただに軍事技術についての知識をえているだけでは不充分という。本書において強調しているところであるが、洋書に記されている軍事技術の叙述に基づいて、これを実際に自己の手で製作してみなければ真に修得したことにはならないとする固い信念である。

彼はこの実証主義、実作主義を徹底させることによって、近代的な学問観を日本社会に定着させるとともに、その実物製作の有用性、有効性の点において彼の学問は卓絶した地位を占めるに至り、勝海舟、吉田松陰ら多くの弟子を門下に集めて教育をほどこし、後世に対して多大の影響を及ぼすこととなった。

これほどに西洋文明の修得に打ち込んだ象山であったが、しかしなお西洋文明に飽き足りぬものを感じていた。西洋の学は自然を研究するに精密であり、精巧なる機械を製作する点において卓越しているが、人間のとらえ方において問題を感じていた。

本来的に朱子学者である象山には儒学の経典である四書五経を捨てることはできなかったし、特に朱子学において強調されていた天人合一の思想—天地自然の現象と人間社会の出来事とは相即するとする思想—や、五倫五常といわれる人倫の根本原則である。彼は本書において、これを、有名な「東洋道徳、西洋芸術」という命題によって定式化する。彼は、西洋学、西洋軍事学を学びに彼の下に入門してきた若い者たちに対して、まず朱子学を修得することを求めていた由である。

象山は欧米の学と近代的な文物を日本国内に系統的に導入していったという点において、日本の近代化を領導した最重要人物の一人であることは疑いのないことであるが、のみならず、「東洋道徳、西洋芸術」という彼の原則は、福沢諭吉の「和魂洋才」論などへと継承、されていくことによって、日本人および東洋人による西洋文明受容のパターンを形成し、日本の近代化の性格規定をなしたという観点において、より一層の重要性

sciences were more advanced. Nevertheless, he recognized fact as fact, and strove to understand those sciences even more positively. And never one to do anything by halves, he even taught himself Dutch. He became fluent in reading original Dutch texts, giving him direct access to the latest information from the West.

Shozan then strove to learn military technology as the source of Western power. What should be noted here is that he was not satisfied just to acquire knowledge of military technology. A point emphasized in this book is his firm conviction that this technology could not be truly acquired without actually trying to reproduce it, based on descriptions in Western literature.

By rigorously applying this policy of demonstration through actual manufacture, Shozan not only established modern scientific attitudes in Japanese society, but his science also rose to an unsurpassed position in terms of the usefulness and effectiveness of making actual objects. He then gathered and educated many pupils, including Katsu Kaishu and Yoshida Shoin, and came to have a tremendous impact on posterity.

But although he was devoted to learning about Western civilization, Shozan still felt there was something missing in it. Western science was precise in its research on nature and unsurpassed in producing elaborate machines, but Shozan sensed a problem in its attitude towards human beings.

As a Neo-Confucian scholar, Shozan could not easily disregard the Four Books and Five Classics, the scriptures of Confucianism. Neo-Confucian learning, in particular, emphasized the "unity of man and heaven" – i.e. the idea that the natural phenomena of heaven and earth are in coalescence with events in human society – and the fundamental tenets of human morality known as "the five human relations and the five virtues". In "Record of Conscience", Shozan formulates this thought in the famous aphorism "Eastern ethics, Western technical learning". This is why the young people who came to learn Western science and Western military technology under his guidance were expected to study Neo-Confucianism first of all.

In that Shozan systematically introduced Western learning and the fruits of modern culture into Japan, there is no doubt that he was one of the most important figures in guiding the modernization of this nation. As well as that, his basic principle of "Eastern ethics, Western technical learning" was inherited by Yukichi Fukuzawa in his doctrine of

を帯びるものと言わなくてはならないであろう。

　今回の紺野先生の英訳本については、象山の原テキストの厳密な文章を最初に提示し、次いでその正確な現代日本語訳本を作成し、そして重要なことに、日本文の一センテンスごとに英訳文章を対応させるという作業を重ねられている点に注意しなければならない。

　愚直にも見える徹底した逐語訳文の作成である。これは、古典文の解釈一般についても言えることなのだが、ともすれば原テキストの難解さを回避して、いわゆる意訳と称する曖昧模糊とした内容で外面だけを取り繕うようなケースを目にすることが少なくない。

　今回の紺野先生の英訳本については、これまでの『啓発録』『留魂録』の二著の英訳で培われた経験をも活かしつつ、逐語訳に徹することによって、象山の原テキストの語義や文意を厳密に英語に移すことに努められている。その真摯な翻訳の態度に敬服するものであり、これによって象山の思想を凝縮した『省諐録』の忠実にして信頼度の高い英訳が完成された。

　さらにまた、紺野先生が各地を回られて渉猟された象山関係の諸資料が本書には多数収録されており、殊に外国圏の方たちにとっては、象山の人となり、また彼の経世論、国防論を理解する縁ともなるだろう。

　かくて佐久間象山『省諐録』の英文テキストとして遺漏の無い書物が公刊される運びとなった。日本からの世界に向けた文化発信という点において誠に意義深いことと、これを心から慶ぶものである。

笠谷和比古

"Japanese spirit, Western technique". In the process, it formed a pattern for acceptance of Western civilization by Japanese and other oriental peoples, and created character rules for the modernization of Japan. Seen from this angle, Sakuma Shozan is surely deserving of even greater notoriety.

An important feature of this English translation by Dr Konno is that he first produced a strict transliteration of Shozan's original text, then converted this accurately into contemporary Japanese, and then, importantly, translated it sentence by sentence into English.

In doing so, Dr Konno has created a strictly literal translation that seems almost too honest. A characteristic seen in interpretations of classic texts in general is that they often tend to avoid the obscure meanings of the original. In doing so, they create a merely superficial impression with a vague and ambiguous content, otherwise known as "liberal translation".

For this English translation, Dr Konno has rigorously insisted on literal translation, drawing partly on the experience amassed in his previous translations of *Keihatsuroku* ("Treatise on Enlightenment") and *Ryūkonroku* ("Soulful Minute"). In this way, he has endeavoured to convert the meanings of words and sentences in Shozan's original text into English. This sincere attitude to translation is to be admired. The result is the publication of a highly reliable English translation, faithful to *Seikenroku* as a condensation of Shozan's thought.

Besides this, Dr Konno has scoured the country for archive materials related to Shozan, many of which are included in this book. For readers in other countries, in particular, these should provide important clues to understanding Shozan's personality, as well as his theories on state affairs and national defence.

And so, this English translation of Sakuma Shozan's *Seikenroku* as "Record of Conscience" has now been published as a book free of omissions. This is not only deeply significant in terms of transmitting culture from Japan to the world, but is also a source of great joy.

Kazuhiko Kasaya

『省諐録』英完訳のための引用文献及び参考文献

1. 信濃教育会編『象山全集』全5巻;信濃毎日新聞社
2. 信濃教育会編『省諐録愆義』昭和5年発行編。
   (飯島忠夫「省諐録に就いて」)
3. 宮本仲『佐久間象山』(岩波版)増訂版復刻:象山社
4. 宮本仲『佐久間象山事績摘要』:岩波書店
5. 大平喜間多『佐久間象山』:日本歴史学会編集:吉川弘文館
6. 大平喜間多『佐久間象山逸話集』:信濃毎日新聞社
7. 前澤英雄『佐久間象山の生涯』:佐久間象山先生顕彰会
8. 田中誠三郎『佐久間象山の実像』銀河書房
9. 佐藤昌介,植手通有,山口宗之『渡辺崋山 高野長英 佐久間象山 横井小楠 橋本左内』日本思想大系 55:岩波書店 (植手通有『省諐録』逐語訳)
   (植手通有:佐久間象山における儒学、武士精神、洋学)
10. 高畑常信,小尾郊一『大塩中斎 佐久間象山』日本の思想家 38:明徳出版
11. 松本健一『評伝 佐久間象山』(上下巻):中公叢書
12. 松浦玲『佐久間象山 横井小楠』日本の名著 30:中央公論社
13. 松浦玲『勝海舟』:筑摩書房
14. 井出孫六『小説 佐久間象山』(上下巻):朝日新聞社
15. 奈良本辰也 左方郁子『佐久間象山』:清水書院
16. 東徹『佐久間象山と科学技術』:思文閣出版
17. 『佐久間象山と象山神社』:象山神社発行
18. 『佐久間象山の世界』:真田宝物館・象山記念館発行
19. 『松代藩と黒船来航』:長野市教育委員会
20. 『真田家の科学技術』:真田宝物館
21. 『佐久間象山とその書』:匠出版
22. 国立史料館『信濃国埴科郡松代伊勢町八田家文書目録』:(その一)
23. 魏源 Wei Yuan『魏源全集』の中の『海国図誌』全50巻:岳麓書社
24. 銭国紅『アジアにおける近代思想の先駆_佐久間象山と魏源』:
    信毎書籍出版センター

Bibliography and References

1. Shinano Kyoiku Kai, eds., *Shōzan Zenshū* ("Complete Works of Shozan"), 5 Volumes, The Shinano Mainichi Shimbun

2. Shinano Kyoiku Kai, eds., *Seikenroku Kengi* ("Moral Guidance in *Seikenroku*"), 1930 Edition (Tadao Iijima, *"Seikenroku ni Tsuite,* "About *Seikenroku*")

3. Chu Miyamoto, *Sakuma Shōzan* (Iwanami Edition), Revised Reprinted Edition, Shozansha

4. Chu Miyamoto, *Sakuma Shōzan Jiseki Tekiyō* ("Summary of Sakuma Shozan's Achievements"), Iwanami Shoten

5. Kimata Ohira, *Sakuma Shōzan*, Nihon Rekishi Gakkai, eds., Yoshikawa Kobunkan

6. Kimata Ohira, *Sakuma Shōzan Itsuwa Shū* ("Collection of Sakuma Shozan Anecdotes"), The Shinano Mainichi Shimbun

7. Hideo Maezawa, *Sakuma Shōzan no Shōgai* ("The Life of Sakuma Shozan"), Sakuma Shozan Sensei Kenshokai

8. Seizaburo Tanaka, *Sakuma Shōzan no Jitsuzō* ("A True Portrait of Sakuma Shozan"), Ginga Shobo

9. Shosuke Sato, Michiari Uete & Muneyuki Yamaguchi, *Watanabe Kazan, Takano Chōei, Sakuma Shōzan, Yokoi Shōnan, Hashimoto Sanai* ("Watanabe Kazan, Takano Choei, Sakuma Shozan, Yokoi Shonan and Hashimoto Sanai"), Nihon Shisō Taikei 55, Iwanami Shoten (*Michiari Uete: Sakuma Shōzan ni Okeru Jugaku, Bushi Seishin, Yōgaku* ("Michiari Uete: Confucianism, Samurai Spirit and Western Learning in Sakuma Shōzan"))

10. Tsunenobu Takahata & Koichi Obi, *Ōshio Chūsai, Sakuma Shōzan* ("Oshio Chusai and Sakuma Shozan"), Nihon no Shisōka 38, Meitoku Shuppan

11. Kenichi Matsumoto, *Hyōden Sakuma Shōzan* ("A Critical Biography of Sakuma Shozan") (Vols. I & II), Chuko Sosho

12. Rei Matsuura, *Sakuma Shōzan, Yokoi Shōnan* ("Sakuma Shozan and Yokoi Shonan"), Nihon no Meicho 30, Chuo Koronsha

13. Rei Matsuura, *Katsu Kaishū*, Chikuma Shobo

14. Magoroku Ide, *Shōsetsu Sakuma Shōzan* ("The Sakuma Shozan Story") (Vols. I & II), Asahi Shimbun Company

15. Tatsuya Naramoto & Fumiko Sakata, *Sakuma Shōzan*, Shimizu Shoin

16. Toru Azuma, *Sakuma Shōzan to Kagaku Gijutsu* ("Sakuma Shozan, Science and Technology"), Shibunkaku Shuppan

17. *Sakuma Shōzan to Zōzan Jinja* ("Sakuma Shozan and Zozan Shrine"), Zozan Jinja

18. *Sakuma Shōzan no Sekai* ("The World of Sakuma Shozan"), Sanada Treasure Museum, Zozan Memorial Hall

25. 『Narrative of the Expedition of an American Squadron on the China Sea and Japan, 1856.』(ペリー艦隊『日本遠征記』上下巻) 翻訳 オフィス宮崎：万来社
26. 飯島忠夫訳注、佐久間象山『省諐録』：岩波文庫
27. 倉田信久『詳解 省愆録』：倉田寛発行
28. 笠谷和比古『近世武家社会の政治構造』：吉川弘文館
29. 笠谷和比古『武士道』侍社会の文化と倫理：NTT 出版
30. 『吉田松陰撰集』(財)松風会。
    特に P.180「三月二十七日夜の記」(回顧録附録)
31. 山川菊栄『覚書 幕末の水戸藩』：岩波文庫
32. 芳賀登『幕末志士の生活』生活史叢書：雄山閣
33. 足立和『ペリー艦隊 黒船に乗っていた日本人』(栄力丸 17 名の漂流人生)：徳間書店
34. 船山馨『定本 幕末の暗殺者；はぐれ雁 佐久間象山暗殺事件』：廣済堂出版
35. 村田犀川『佐久間象山言行録』偉人研究 35：内外出版協会
36. 井野辺茂雄『幕末史の研究』(佐久間象山の対外意見)：雄山閣
37. 萩原裕雄『江戸幕閣人物 100 話』：立風書房
38. 大庭三郎『佐久間象山百話』教訓叢書：求光閣
39. 森滄浪『東湖・象山・松陰・小楠幕末四傑』(学風管見)：金鶏学院
40. 金子鷹之助解題『高島秋帆・佐久間象山』(近世社会経済学説大系)：誠文堂新光社
41. 金子鷹之助『熊沢蕃山と佐久間象山』(ラジオ新書)：日本放送協会
42. 波多野通敏『佐久間象山の武士道』(道義叢書)：青年教育普及会
43. 増沢淑『科学の先駆者 佐久間象山』：日本書房
44. 中沢護人『幕末の思想家』(佐久間象山と横井小楠__主知)：筑摩書房
45. 徳富蘇峰『歴史の証言』：国民新報社編
46. 徳富猪一郎『吉田松陰』：東京民友社
47. 綱淵謙錠『血と血糊のあいだ』(佐久間象山の自意識)：河出書房新社
48. 信夫清三郎『象山と松陰__開国と攘夷の論理__』：河出書房新社
49. 佐藤昌介『洋学史の研究』(佐久間象山と蘭学)：中央公論社 1980

19. *Matsushiro Han to Kurofune Raikō* ("The Matsushiro Domain and the Perry Expedition"), Nagano City Board of Education

20. *Sanada-ke no Kagaku Gijutsu* ("Science and Technology of the Sanada Family"), Sanada Treasure Museum

21. *Sakuma Shōzan to Sono Sho* ("Sakuma Shozan and his Writings"), Takumi Shuppan

22. Department of Historical Documents, *Shinano Kuni Hanishina-gun Matsushiro Isemachi Hatta-ke Monjo Mokuroku* ("Document Inventory of the Hatta Family of Matsushiro Isemachi, Hanishina County in Shinano Province") (Part I)

23. Wei Yuan, *Haiguo Tuzhi* ("Illustrated Treatise on the Maritime Kingdoms") in *Weiyuan Quanji* ("Complete Works of Wei Yuan"), 50 Volumes, Yuelu Publishing House

24. Qian Guohong, *Ajia ni Okeru Kindai Shisō no Sakigake: Sakuma Shōzan to Gi Gen* ("Pioneers of Modern Thought in Asia: Sakuma Shozan and Wei Yuan"), Shinmai Shoseki Shuppan Senta

25. Narrative of the Expedition of an American Squadron on the China Sea and

    Japan, 1856 (Vols. I & II), Transl. Office Miyazaki, Banraisha

26. Tadao Iijima, Annotated Translation, *Sakuma Shōzan Seikenroku* ("Record of Conscience by Sakuma Shozan"), Iwanami Bunko

27. Nobuhisa Kurata, *Shōkai Seikenroku* ("Record of Conscience: A Detailed Analysis"), Hiroshi Kurata

28. Kazuhiko Kasaya, *Kinsei Buke Shakai no Seiji Kōzō* ("Political Structure of Premodern Samurai Society"), Yoshikawa Kobunkan

29. Kazuhiko Kasaya, *Bushidō – Samurai Shakai no Bunka to Rinri* ("Culture and Ethics of Samurai Society"), NTT Publishing Co., Ltd

30. *Yoshida Shōin Senshū* ("Yoshida Shoin Anthology"), Shofukai, particularly p.180 *Sangatsu Nijūshichinichi Yoru no Ki* ("Account of the Night of March 27", Memoir Appendix)

31. Kikue Yamakawa, *Oboegaki Bakumatsu to Mito Han* ("Notes on the Mito Domain in the Bakumatsu Period"), Iwanami Bunko

32. Noboru Haga, *Bakumatsu Shishi no Seikatsu* ("How the Bakumatsu Patriots Lived"), Seikatsushi Sosho, Yuzankaku

33. Yawara Adachi, *Perī Kantai ni Notte ita Nihonjin* ("Japanese Who Boarded Perry's Fleet") (Lives of the 17 Eiriki Maru Castaways), Tokuma Shoten Publishing

34. Kaoru Funayama, *Teihon Bakumatsu no Ansatsusha: Haguregan Sakuma Shōzan Ansatsu Jiken* ("Revised Edition, Bakumatsu Assassins: The Assassination of 'Lone Goose' Sakuma Shozan"), Kosaido Publishing

35. Kankei Murata, *Sakuma Shōzan Genkōroku* ("Record of Words and Deeds by Sakuma Shozan"), Ijin Kenkyū 35, Naigai Shuppan Kyokai

36. Shigeo Inobe, *Bakumatsushi no Kenkyū* ("Research on Bakumatsu

50. ドナルド・キーン『百代の過客＿＿日記に見る日本人』下巻：朝日選書
51. 林青梧『江川太郎左衛門＿＿開国派英才 挫折す』(傀儡・佐久間象山)：
    読売新聞社
52. 杉田幸三『幕末ものしり読本』(メカに強い佐久間象山)：廣済堂出版
53. 中西進『非凡者 光と影』(佐久間象山)：時事通信社
54. 宮崎市定『古代大和朝廷』
    (幕末の攘夷論と開国論〜佐久間象山暗殺の背景)：筑摩書房
55. 子母澤寛『幕末奇談』(佐久間象山の倅) 文春文庫：文芸春秋
56. 諸田玲子『お順』(勝海舟の妹と五人の男)：毎日新聞社
57. 源了圓『佐久間象山』(歴史人物シリーズ 幕末維新の群像第8巻)：
    PHP研究所
58. 黒岩俊郎『技術の文化史』(関 章{佐久間象山と日本の電気技術の遺産})：
    アグネ
59. 中沢至夫『史説 幕末暗殺』(彦斎、佐久間象山を斬る)：雄山閣
60. 松本健一『維れ新たなり』：講演集1．：人間と歴史社
61. 松本健一『開国のかたち』：毎日新聞社
62. 江戸漢詩選『志士 藤田東湖 佐久間象山 橋本左内 吉田松陰 西郷隆盛』：岩波書店
63. 紺野大介 橋本左内著『啓発録』英完訳書：錦正社
64. 紺野大介 吉田松陰著『留魂録』英完訳書：錦正社
65. 島崎藤村『夜明け前』：新潮社
66. 大江孝之「佐久間象山翁の長歌」：東洋学芸雑誌 1883
67. 北沢正誠「象山と松陰＿＿品川子爵談」：太陽 5-18, 1899
68. 三味居士「佐久間象山 久坂玄瑞 山県半蔵の会見」：防長史談会雑誌 1-1, 1909
69. 増沢淑「佐久間象山の理化学研究」：地理歴史教育 2-9, 1930
70. 佐藤寅太郎「政治家としての佐久間象山」：信濃教育 562, 1933
71. 町田生「平賀源内の発電機と松代公」：信濃 1-3-7 1934
72. 高見沢忠雄「佐久間象山の国防論策」：長崎談義 21, 1937

History") (Sakuma Shozan's Views on External Affairs), Yuzankaku

37. Yasuo Hagiwara, *Edo Bakkaku Jinbutsu Hyakuwa* ("A Hundred Tales of Top Edo Officials"), Rippu Shobo Publishing

38. Saburo Oba, *Sakuma Shōzan Hyakuwa* ("A Hundred Tales of Sakuma Shozan"), Kyokun Sosho, Kyukokaku

39. Soro Mori, *Tōko, Shōzan, Shōin, Shōnan: Bakumatsu Shiketsu (Gakufū Kanken)* ("Toko, Shozan, Shoin, Shonan: Four Bakumatsu Greats (A Scholarly View)"), Kinkei Gakuin

40. Takanosuke Kaneko, Commentary, *Takashima Shūhan, Sakuma Shōzan (Kinsei Shakai Keizai Gakusetsu Taikei)* ("Takashima Shuhan, Sakuma Shozan (Compendium of Premodern Socio-Economic Theory)"), Seibundo Shinkosha Publishing

41. Takanosuke Kaneko, *Kumazawa Banzan to Sakuma Shōzan (Rajio Shinsho)* ("Kumazawa Banzan and Sakuma Shozan (Radio Shinsho)"), NHK (Japan Broadcasting Corporation)

42. Michitoshi Hatano, *Sakuma Shōzan no Bushidō (Dōgi Sosho)* ("Sakuma Shozan's Bushido (Monograph on Morality)"), Seinen Kyoiku Fukyukai

43. Kiyoshi Masuzawa, *Kagaku no Senkusha Sakuma Shōzan* ("Sakuma Shozan, Pioneer of Science"), Nihon Shobo

44. Morito Nakazawa, *Bakumatsu no Shisōka (Sakuma Shōzan to Yokoi Shōnan – Shuchi)* ("Bakumatsu Thinkers (Sakuma Shozan and Yokoi Shonan: Intellectualism)"), Chikuma Shobo

45. Soho Tokutomi, *Rekishi no Shōgen* ("Testimony of History"), Kokumin Shinbunsha, eds.

46. Iichiro Tokutomi, *Yoshida Shōin*, Tokyo Minyusha

47. Kenjo Tsunabuchi, *Chi to Chinori no Aida* ("Between Blood and Gore") (Sakuma Shozan's Self-Awareness), Kawade Shobo Shinsha

48. Seizaburo Shinobu, *Shōzan to Sōin: Kaikoku to Jōi no Ronri* ("Shozan and Soin: The Policies of Ending National Isolation and Expelling Foreigners"), Kawade Shobo Shinsha

49. Shosuke Sato, *Yōgakushi no Kenkyū* ("Research on the History of Western Studies") (Sakuma Shozan and Dutch Studies), Chuo Koronsha

50. Donald Keene, *Travelers of a Hundred Ages: The Japanese As Revealed Through 1,000 Years of Diaries*, Vol. 2, Asahi Sensho

51. Seigo Hayashi, *Egawa Tarōzaemon: Kaikokuha Eisai Zasetsusu (Kairai Sakuma Shozan)* ("Egawa Tarozaemon: A Setback for a Brilliant Advocate of Westernization), Yomiuri Shimbunsha

52. Kozo Sugita, *Bakumatsu Monoshiri Dokuhon* ("Reader on the Bakumatsu Sages") (Sakuma Shozan's Ability in Mechanical Matters), Kosaido Publishing

53. Susumu Nakanishi, *Hibonsha: Hikari to Kage (Sakuma Shozan)* ("Outstanding Figures: Light and Shade"), Jiji Press Ltd.

54. Ichisada Miyazaki, *Kodai Yamato Chōtei* ("The Ancient Yamato Court")

73. 柳沢平助「象山佐久間先生と力士雷電為右衛門」:信濃教育 626, 1938
74. 宮本璋「佐久間象山の洋学について」:日本医事新報 646-648, 1938
75. 内田周平「佐久間象山の学術に就いて」:国史回顧会紀要 39, 1939
76. 池田哲郎「佐久間象山と蘭学」:福島大学学芸学部論集 第10号、1959
77. 池田哲郎「象山蘭語彙__佐久間象山の使用したオランダ語」:
    蘭学資料研究会報告 1959
78. 高橋宏「佐久間象山 雅号呼称の決め手」:信州大学教養学部紀要
    第29号,1995
79. 北島正元「佐久間象山の科学思想」:歴史日本 1944
80. 中沢護人「和魂洋才と東西両洋の仲裁人_象山・松陰・左内と内村鑑三」:
    思想の科学 1961
81. 鬼頭有一「格別制器論考_佐久間象山における儒学と科学の対決」:
    東洋文化 8, 1962
82. 塚田正明「佐久間象山の女性観」:信濃教育 935、1964
83. 丸山眞男「幕末における視座の改革」:展望77 5月号 筑摩書房 1965
84. 小林計一郎「コレラと佐久間象山」:日本の歴史 200 1965
85. 山崎馨「黒川良安と佐久間象山」:大阪大学医療技術短大学部研究紀要人
    文科学編 1970
86. 松浦玲「架空問答 横井小楠と佐久間象山」:中央公論臨時増刊
    歴史と人物 1971
87. 清水憲雄「象山の恋文」:信濃教育 1034, 1971
88. 布施光男「佐久間象山の電気治療器について」:蘭学資料研究会研究報告
    298, 1975
89. 坂本保富「東洋道徳・西洋芸術における教育認識と特質」:東京教育大研究
    収録 16,1976
90. 川尻信夫「幕末西洋数学受容の一断面_象山の「詳証術」をめぐって」:思想
    628, 1976
91. 川尻信夫「幕末におけるヨーロッパ学術受容の一断面」:東海大学出版会
    1982

(Bakumatsu Theories of Expelling Foreigners and Westernization – Background to the Assassination of Sakuma Shozan), Chikuma Shobo

55. Kan Shimozawa, *Bakumatsu Kidan* ("Bakumatsu Anecdotes") (Sakuma Shozan's Son), Bunshu Bunko, Bungei Shunju Ltd.

56. Reiko Morota, *O-Jun – Katsu Kaishū no Imōto to Gonin no Otoko* ("O-Jun – Katsu Kaishu's Younger Sister and Five Men"), The Mainichi Newspapers Co., Ltd.

57. Ryoen Minamoto, *Sakuma Shōzan* (Historical Figures Series: *Bakumatsu Ishin no Gunzō Dai Hachi Kan* ("Group Portrait from the Bakumatsu and Meiji Restoration Vol. 8")), PHP Research Institute

58. Toshiro Kuroiwa, *Gijutsu no Bunkashi* ("Cultural History of Technology") (Akira Seki, *Sakuma Shōzan to Nihon no Denki Gijutsu no Isan* ("Sakuma Shozan and the Heritage of Japan's Electric Technology")), Agne Gijutsu Center

59. Michio Nakazawa, *Shisetsu – Bakumatsu Ansatsu* ("Historical Theory: Bakumatsu Assassinations") (Gensai Kills Sakuma Shozan), Yuzankaku

60. Kenichi Matsumoto, *Kore Aratanari* ("Amend and Make New: Restoration"), Lecture Series 1., Ningen to Rekishi Sha

61. Kenichi Matsumoto, *Kaikoku no Katachi* ("The Shape of Westernization") (Sakuma Shozan's View on the Significance of Perry's Expedition, etc.), The Mainichi Newspapers Co., Ltd.

62. Selection of Edo Chinese Poetry, *Shishi: Fujita Tōko, Sakuma Shōzan, Hashimoto Sanai, Yoshida Shōin, Saigō Takamori* ("Patriots: Fujita Toko, Sakuma Shozan, Hashimoto Sanai, Yoshida Shoin and Saigo Takamori"), Iwanami Shoten

63. Daisuke Konno, *Treatise on Enlightenment* (English Translation of *Keihatsuroku* by Hashimoto Sanai), Kinseisha

64. Daisuke Konno, *Soulful Minute* (English Translation of *Ryūkonroku* by Yoshida Shoin), Kinseisha

65. Toson Shimazaki, *Yoake Mae* ("Before the Dawn"), Shinchosha

66. Takayuki Oe, *Sakuma Shōzan Okina No Nagauta* ("Nagauta Poems by Sakuma Shozan"), Toyo Gakugei Zasshi, 1883

67. Masanari Kitazawa, *Shōzan to Shōin: Shinagawa Shishaku Dan* ("Shozan and Shoin: Conversation with Shinagawa Shishaku"), Taiyo 5-18, 1899

68. Yasutomi Sakamoto, *Kome Hyappyō no Shujinkō Kobayashi Torasaburō* ("Kobayashi Torasaburo, Protagonist of the One Hundred Bags of Rice"), Gakubunsha

69. Kiyoshi Masuzawa, *Sakuma Shōzan no Rikagaku Kenkyū* ("Sakuma Shozan's Research in Physics and Chemistry"), Chiri Rekishi Kyoiku 2-9, 1930

70. Torataro Sato, *Seijika Toshite no Sakuma Shōzan* ("Sakuma Shozan as a Politician"), Shinano Kyoiku 562, 1933

71. Machida Sho, *Hiraga Gennai no Hatsudenki to Matsushiro Kō* ("Hiraga

92. 吉羽和夫「技術遺産の探訪_10_佐久間象山の電信実験」:技術と人間 7-7, 1978
93. 市川本太郎「佐久間象山と漢学～特に漢詩について」:長野 92、1980
94. 内田与一「象山の妻妾について」:長野 92, 1980
95. 八田勇「信濃国植科郡松代伊勢町八田家文書目録その 1」:国立資料館 1985
96. 杉本つとむ 佐久間象山『増訂荷蘭語彙』の小察 :日本歴史 415, 1982
97. 栗原孝 近世「鬼神論」の政治思想史的意味_白石・篤胤・象山をめぐって:桐朋学園大学研究紀要 9, 1983
98. 飯田鼎「幕末知識人の西欧認識_佐久間象山と福沢諭吉」:三田学会雑誌 77-1, 1984
99. 藪内清・宗田一「江戸時代の科学器械」:恒星社 1964
100. 関 章「佐久間象山の電池___再現と実験」:産業考古学 34, 1984
101. 関 章「佐久間象山の電信実験」:産業考古学 32, 1984
102. 古川学「インド大反乱と佐久間象山」:史学 55-4, 1986
103. 斎藤利生「横浜の２門の洋砲」:防衛大学校紀要（人文科学）53, 1986
104. 井口朝生「白昼の斬人剣」_佐久間象山暗殺:別冊歴史読本（新人物往来社）1988
105. 三上一夫「横井小楠・佐久間象山の海防論 両論の異同性」:福井工大研究紀要 1993
106. 大橋敦夫 佐久間象山『増訂荷蘭語彙』出版計画をめぐって:真田宝物館 8, 1995
107. 大橋敦夫 新出資料『五車韻府』をめぐって 同上松代:真田宝物館 9, 1996
108. 佐久間方三「佐久間象山の漢詩」1~6.市誌研究ながの:16~21, 2009～2015
109. 王暁秋「幕末の日米条約交渉に立ち会った中国人羅森」:現代中国事情 2008.3
110. 王暁秋「中国人の目から見た近代中日文化交流年表」:国際基督教大学学報 2009,3

Gennai's Electricity Generator and the Lord of Matsushiro"), Shinano 1-3-7, 1934

72. Tadao Takamizawa, *Sakuma Shōzan no Kokubō Ronsaku* ("Sakuma Shozan's Treatise on National Defence"), Nagasaki Dangi 21, 1937

73. Heisuke Yanagisawa, *Shōzan Sakuma Sensei to Rikishi Raidentaemon* ("Sakuma Shozan and the Wrestler Raidentaemon"), Shinano Kyoiku 626, 1938

74. Akira Miyamoto, *Sakuma Shōzan no Yōgaku ni Tsuite* ("On Sakuma Shozan's Western Studies"), Japan Medical Journal 646-648, 1938

75. Shuhei Uchida, *Sakuma Shōzan no Gakujutsu ni Tsuite* ("On Sakuma Shozan's Learning"), Kokushi Kaikokai Kiyo 39, 1939

76. Tetsuro Ikeda, *Sakuma Shōzan to Rangaku* ("Sakuma Shozan and Dutch Studies"), Bulletin of the Faculty of Liberal Arts, Fukushima University No.10, 1959

77. Tetsuro Ikeda, *Shōzan Rangoi: Sakuma Shōzan no Shiyō Shita Oranda-go* ("Shozan's Dutch Vocabulary: Dutch Language as Used by Sakuma Shozan"), Rangaku Shiryo Kenkyukai Kenkyu Hokoku, 1959

78. Hiroshi Takahashi, *Sakuma Shōzan – Gagō Koshō no Kimete* ("Sakuma Shozan: Reasons for Deciding Pseudonyms"), Journal of the Faculty of Liberal Arts and Science, Shinshu University No. 29, 1995

79. Masamoto Kitajima, *Sakuma Shōzan no Kagaku Shisō* ("Scientific Thought of Sakuma Shozan"), Rekishi Nihon, 1944

80. Morito Nakazawa, *Wakon Yōsai to Tōzai Ryōyō no Chūsainin – Shōzan, Shōin, Sanai to Uchimura Kanzō* ("Mediators between Japanese Spirit and Western Technique, East and West – Shozan, Shoin, Sanai and Uchimura Kanzo"), Shiso no Kagaku, 1961

81. Yuichi Kito, *Kakubetsu Seikironkō – Sakuma Shōzan ni Okeru Jugaku to Kagaku no Taiketsu* ("Discussion of Exceptional Control Devices– The Collision of Confucianism and Science in Sakuma Shozan"), Toyo Bunka 8, 1962

82. Masaaki Tsukada, *Sakuma Shōzan no Joseikan* ("Sakuma Shozan's Views on Women"), Shinano Kyoiku 935, 1964

83. Masao Maruyama, *Bakumatsu ni Okeru Shiza no Kaikaku* ("Changing Perspectives in the Bakumatsu Period"), Tenbo 77 May issue, Chikuma Shobo, 1965

84. Keiichiro Kobayashi, *Korera to Sakuma Shōzan* ("Cholera and Sakuma Shozan"), Nihon no Rekishi 200, 1965

85. Kaoru Yamazaki, *Kurokawa Masayasu to Sakuma Shōzan* ("Kurokawa Masayasu and Sakuma Shozan"), Studies in the Humanities, Research Bulletin of Osaka University College of Bio-Medical Technology, 1970

86. Rei Matsuura, *Kakū Mondō: Yokoi Shōnan to Sakuma Shōzan* ("An Imaginary Dialogue: Yokoi Shonan and Sakuma Shozan"), Chuo Koron Extra Edition, Rekishi to Jinbutsu, 1971

87. Norio Shimizu, *Shōzan no Renbun* ("Shozan's Love Letters"), Shinano

111. 近代日本総合年表 第三版 :岩波書店

Kyoiku 1034, 1971

88. Mitsuo Fuse, *Sakuma Shōzan no Denki Chiryōki ni Tsuite* ("On Sakuma Shozan's Electric Therapy Machine"), Rangaku Shiryo Kenkyukai Kenkyu Hokoku 298, 1975

89. Yasutomi Sakamoto, *Tōyō Dōtoku, Saiyō Geijutsu ni Okeru Kyōiku Ninshiki to Tokushitsu* ("Educational Perceptions and Characteristics in Oriental Morality and Western Art"), Tokyo University of Education Research Records 16, 1976

90. Nobuo Kawajiri, *Bakumatsu Seiyō Sūgaku Juyō no Ichidanmen – Shōzan no 'Shōshōjutsu' wo Megutte* ("A Cross-Section of Receptiveness to Western Mathematics in Bakumatsu Japan: Focusing on Shozan's 'Probative Science'"), Shiso 628, 1976

91. Nobuo Kawajiri, *Bakumatsu ni Okeru Yōroppa Gakujutsu Juyō no Ichidanmen* ("A Cross-Section of Receptiveness to European Learning in Bakumatsu Japan"), Tokai University Press, 1982

92. Kazuo Yoshiba, *Gijutsu Isan no Tanbō – 10: Sakuma Shōzan no Denshin Jikken* ("The Search for Technology Heritage – 10: Sakuma Shozan's Experiments in Telecommunications"), Gijutsu to Ningen 7-7, 1978

93. Mototaro Ichikawa, *Sakuma Shōzan to Kangaku – Toku ni Kanshi ni Tsuite* ("Sakuma Shozan and Confucianism – With Particular Focus on Chinese Poetry"), Nagano 92, 1980

94. Yoichi Uchida, *Shōzan no Saishō ni Tsuite* ("On Shōzan's Wife and Mistresses"), Nagano 92, 1980

95. Takeo Itazawa, *Shīboruto* ("Siebold"), Nihon Rekishi Gakkai, eds., Yoshikawa Kobunkan

96. Tsutomu Sugimoto, *Sakuma Shōzan "Zōteini Rangoi" no Kosatsu* ("Examination of Sakuma Shozan's 'Revised and Enlarged Dutch Dictionary'"), Nihon Rekishi 415, 1982

97. Takashi Kurihara, *Kinsei "Kishinron" no Seiji Shisōshi Teki Imi – Shiraishi, Atsutane, Shōzan wo Megutte* ("Implications of the Premodern 'Theory of Demons and Deities' for the History of Political Thought: With Focus on Shiraishi, Atsutane and Shozan"), Toho Gakuen School of Music Research Bulletin 9, 1983

98. Kanae Iida, *Bakumatsu Chishikijin no Seiō Ninshiki – Sakuma Shōzan to Fukuzawa Yukichi* ("Western Perceptions of Bakumatsu Intellectuals: Sakuma Shozan and Fukuzawa Yukichi"), Mita Journal of Economics 77-1, 1984

99. Kiyoshi Yabuuchi & Hajime Soda, *Edo Jidai no Kagaku Kikai* ("Scientific Instruments in the Edo Period"), Koseisha, 1964

100. Akira Seki, *Sakuma Shōzan no Denchi – Saigen to Jikken* ("Sakuma Shozan's Batteries – Reconstruction and Experiments"), Industrial Archaeology 34, 1984

101. Akira Seki, *Sakuma Shōzan no Denshin Jikken* ("Sakuma Shozan's Experiments in Telecommunications"), Industrial Archaeology 32, 1984

102. Satoru Furukawa, *Indo Daihanran to Sakuma Shōzan* ("The Great

Mutiny in India and Zozan Sakuma"), Shigaku 55-4, 1986

103. Toshio Saito, *Yokohama no 2-Mon no Yōhō* ("The Two Western Cannons at Yokohama"), Bulletin of the National Defense Academy (Humanities Series) 53, 1986

104. Asao Iguchi, *"Hakuchū no Zanninken" – Sakuma Shōzan Ansatsu: Bessatsu Rekishi Dokuhon* ("'The Assassin's Sword in Broad Daylight' – Assassination of Sakuma Shozan: History Reader Supplement") Shinjinbutsu Oraisha, 1988

105. Kazuo Mikami, *Yokoi Shōnan, Sakuma Shōzan no Kaibōron – Ryōron no Idōsei* ("Naval Defence Theories of Yokoi Shonan and Sakuma Shozan – Differences and Similarities"), Memoirs of Fukui University of Technology, 1993

106. Atsuo Ohashi, *Sakuma Shōzan "Zōteini Rangoi" Shuppan Keikaku wo Megutte* ("On Sakuma Shozan's Plan to Publish the 'Revised and Enlarged Dutch Dictionary'"), Sanada Treasure Museum 8, 1995

107. Atsuo Ohashi, *Shinshutsu Shiryō "Wu Che Yun Fu" wo Megutte* ("On the Newly Reproduced 'Dictionary of the Chinese Language'"), *ibidem*, Matsushiro Sanada Treasure Museum 9, 1996

108. Masami Sakuma, *Sakuma Shōzan no Kanshi* ("Sakuma Shozan's Chinese Poetry") 1-6, Shishi Kenkyū Nagano 16-21, 2009-2015

109. Wang Xiaoqiu, *Bakumatsu no Nichibei Jōyaku Kōshō ni Tachiatta Chūgokujin Ra Shin* ("Luo Sen, Chinese Interpreter who Attended the Japan-US Treaty Negotiations in the Bakumatsu Era"), Gendai Chugoku Jijo, March 2008

110. Wang Xiaoqiu, *Chūgokujin no Me Kara Mita Kindai Chūnichi Bunka Kōryū Nenpyō* ("Chronology of Modern Sino-Japanese Cultural Exchanges Through the Eyes of the Chinese"), Academic Reports of the International Christian University 2009, 3

111. *Kindai Nihon Sōgō Nenpyō* ("General Chronology of Modern Japan"), 3rd Edition, Iwanami Shoten

著者略歴

紺野大介

　科学技術者、企業経営者、大学教授、論説随筆家、幕末維新歴史研究家。1945年生まれ。東京大学で流体力学・流体工学を中心に自然科学を学び、工学博士の学位を取得。この間、旧ソ連Moscow大学数理統計研究所に短期留学。また野村／Harvard Management Schoolで「トップのための経営戦略講座」修得。1999年まで日本の重厚長大及び軽薄短小型の大企業2社で研究開発本部長、新規事業本部長、取締役CTOなど重責を担った。

　併任で日本機械学会論文審査委員、通産省・大型国家プロジェクト作業部会長、政令指定都市・新潟市の市長顧問、最近では政府創設の国策会社「産業革新機構」創立時 key person として参画、初代取締役・産業革新委員など歴任。2000年以来今日まで1200名余の評価委員を擁する技術事業性評価のための公益シンクタンクETTの理事長＆CEOを務める。また自民党、民主党の主流国会議員団の要請により「中国の動静」などについて講演。1994年以来、中国・清華大学・SKLT（摩擦学国家重点実験室）招聘教授、2008年からは北京大学・RICFRH（歴史学系中外関係史研究所）客座教授も務める。中国を代表するTop 2大学の双方で教授職にある現在日本で唯一の人物でもあり中国要人とのパイプも太い。また伝統ある日中科学技術交流協会常務理事も兼ねている。

　一方、世界70ケ国を学術・ビジネスで歴訪。傍ら英国Cambridge大学など数大学、仏国CEEJA（欧州日本学研究所）など海外の日本研究機関で武士道等に関する招待講演を実施。こうした体験を基に、世界に日本を理解戴くため日本人のエートス、価値観、閉鎖性、謙虚さ、潔さ、美意識等を幕末維新期の偉人に素材を求め、その著作を英完訳し海外大学や研究機関等に無償で配布・紹介している。1996年上梓された第一作目の橋本左内『啓発録』英訳書は、同年米国クリントン大統領から感謝状を授与。2003年の吉田松陰『留魂録』英訳書に続き、本書の佐久間象山『省諐録』英訳書は第三作目となる。他に著作『中国の頭脳・清華大学と北京大学』（朝日新聞）、『民度革命のすすめ』（東邦出版）等がある。

　氏はこの著の巻末にあるようにOvidによるラテン語の下記の諺を好み原則的な生活信条にしている。

Bene qui latuit, bene vixit
「よく隠れし者は、よく生きたり！」

{意}　世の波に浮かび、風に消える声をたてる必要はない。
　　　海深く沈み、波を起こすことが大事である。
　　　誰にも知られないで、誰もが動かされるような。

Author Profile

Daisuke KONNO

Japanese Scientist, Engineer, Business Director ,Professor, Essayist and Editorial writer, and Researcher on the history of Japan's Bakumatsu period and Meiji Restoration.

Born in 1945, Dr. Konno studied engineering (with particular focus on fluid dynamics and fluid engineering) at the University of Tokyo, eventually earning a Ph.D. in Mechanical Engineering. In the meantime, he went abroad for short-term study at the Mathematical Statistics Institute of Moscow University in the former Soviet Union. He also attended the "Top Management Course" at the Nomura Harvard Management School.

Until 1999, he filled important positions such as Division Executive, Board Member and CTO in listed Japanese companies of all conceivable sizes. In the past, he concurrently held other posts including Reviewer of Papers for the Japan Society of Mechanical Engineering, Chair of the National Big Project at MITI, and more recently, the first Director as well as Industrial Innovation Committee Member and others as the key person and prime mover upon the creation of the national corporation "Innovation Network Corporation of Japan" by the Japanese government.

Since 2000, he has served as President and CEO of the Eureka Think Tank for evaluation of technical projects, an organization with over 1,200 evaluators. Concurrently, as Political Counselor to the Mayor of Niigata City, he has given lectures on "China's Movements" and other subjects upon request by prominent Dietmembers' groups from the Liberal Democratic Party and the Democratic Party.

Since 1994, he has served as Tenured Professor, State Key Laboratory on Tribology at Tsinghua University in China, and since 2008 as Guest Professor, RICFRH of History Dept. at Peking University. This makes him the only Japanese person to hold professorial posts at both of China's top two universities, and has yielded strong connections with high-ranking Chinese officials. He also serves as General Executive Board Member and Director of the Japan-China Science & Technology Exchange Association.

Meanwhile, he has visited 70 of the world's countries for academic or business purposes, and has given lectures on Bushido (The Way of the Samurai) at Cambridge University in England and other universities, European Center for Japanese studies, Alsace in France and elsewhere. To increase understanding of Japan in the world, he looks for Japanese attributes such as their ethos, reservedness, values, humility, graciousness, and aesthetic awareness in the great figures of the Bakumatsu and Meiji Restoration period, then translates their works into English and distributes or introduces them free at overseas universities and elsewhere. He received a letter of acknowledgement from US President Clinton for the first of these, the English translation of *Keihatsuroku* ("Treatise on Enlightenment") by Hashimoto Sanai, published in 1996. The second was *Ryūkonroku* ("Soulful Minute") by Yoshida Shoin, published in 2003, followed now by the third, *Seikenroku* ("Record of Conscience") by Sakuma Shozan.

Other publications include *Chūgoku no Zunō – Seika Daigaku to Pekin Daigaku* ("Brains of China – Tsinghua and Peking Universities", Asahi Shimbun) and *Mindo Kakumei no Susume* ("Encouragement for Revolution in Cultural Standards", Toho Publishing).

Of these previous publications, *Mindo Kakumei no Susume* ends with a
  Latin quotation from a poem by Ovid (43BC–17AD):

> *Bene qui latuit, bene vixit*
> "He who hid well, lived well"

To paraphrase:
  We have no need to flow with the tide or shout into the wind.
  Better to conceal ourselves in the depths and make waves from there.
  Unknown by all, but causing all to move.

This is Dr. Konno's principle life creed.

佐久間象山著「省諐録」英完訳書
"Record of Conscience"

平成28年3月27日　印刷
平成28年4月15日　発行

※定価は函等に表示してあります。

訳　者　　紺野大介
装丁者　　吉野史門
発行者　　中藤正道
発行所　　㈱錦正社
〒162-0041　東京都新宿区早稲田鶴巻町544-6
TEL　03（5261）2891
FAX　03（5261）2892
URL　http://www.kinseisha.jp/

落丁本・乱丁本はお取替えいたします。　　印刷・㈱平河工業社　製本・㈱ブロケード
Ⓒ 2016 Printed in Japan　　　　　　　　　ISBN978-4-7646-0125-3

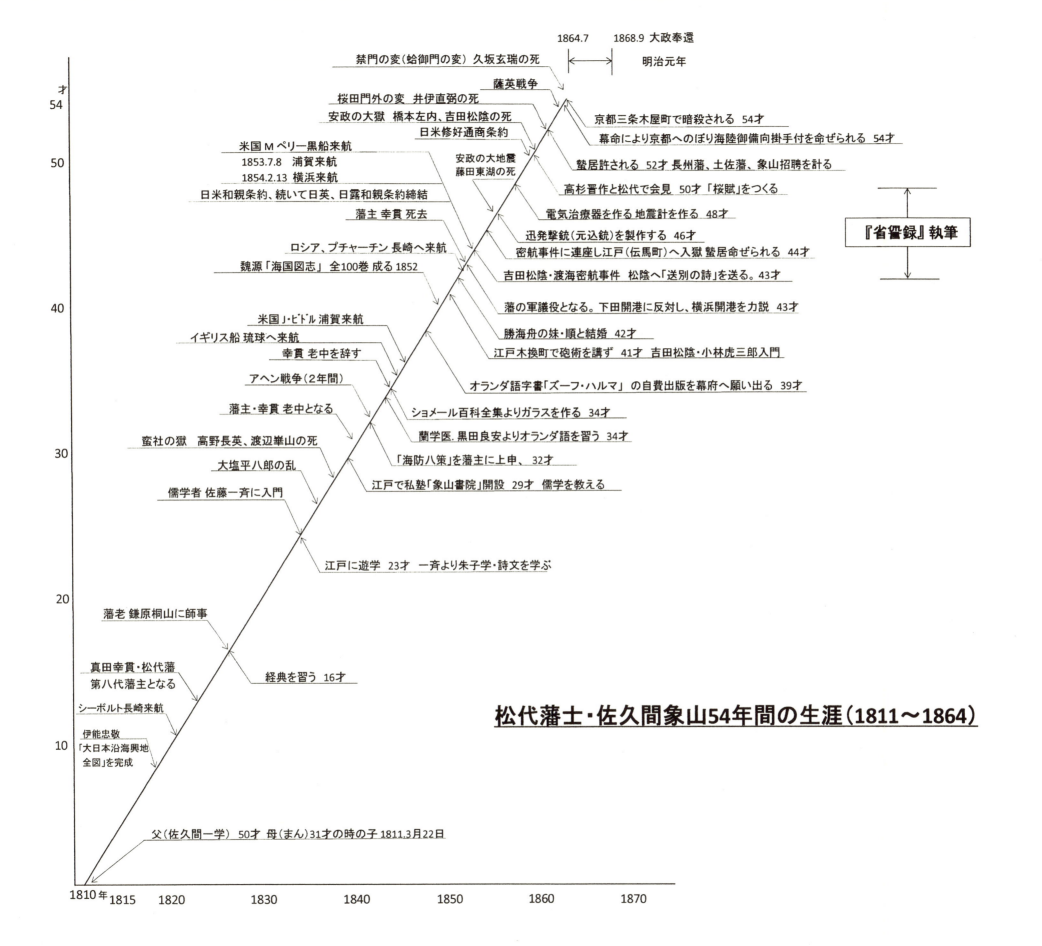

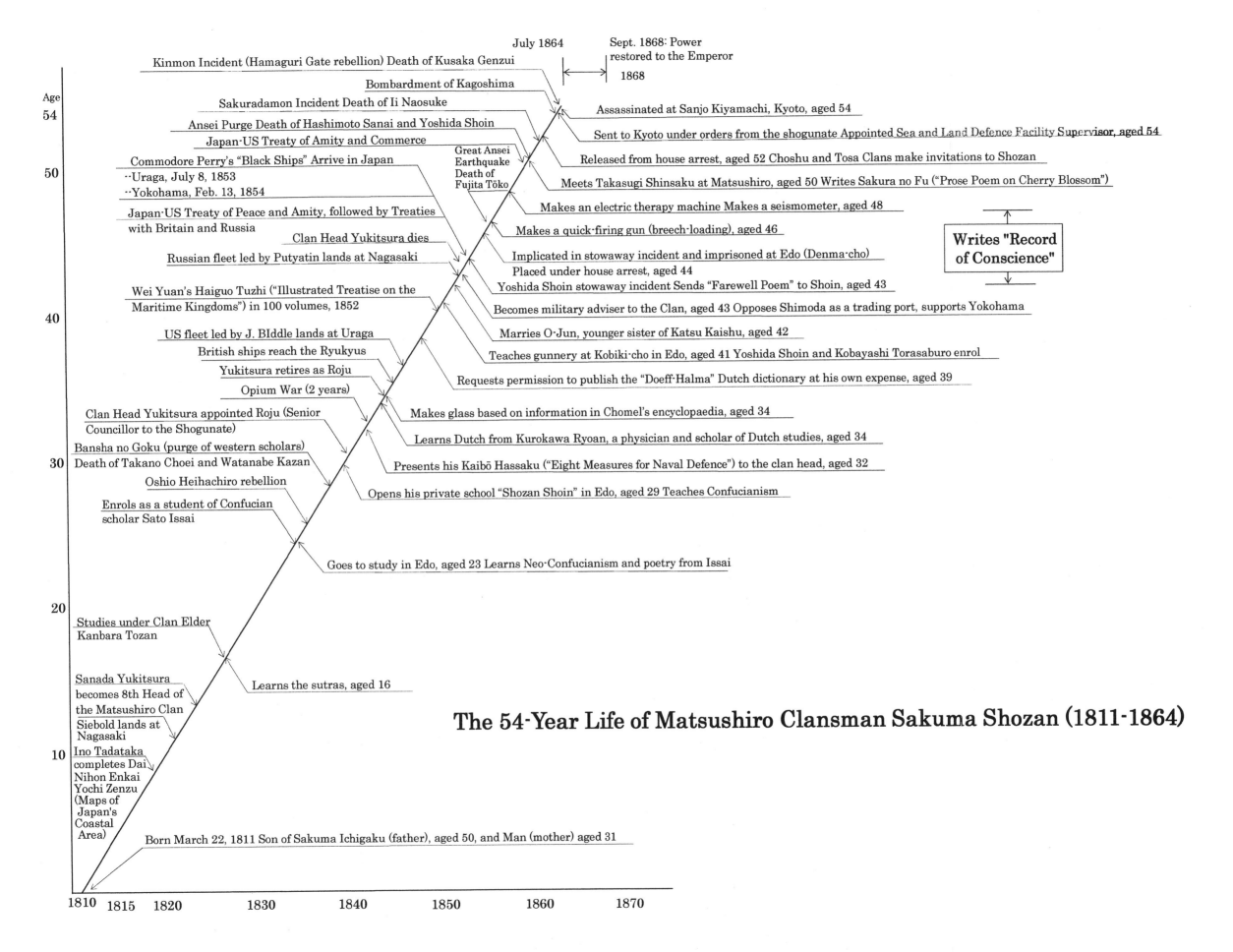